I KNOW A YOUNG WOMAN WHO

God Songs from *O[dd*

By Dr Hazel But[ler

In this unique and exciting new book, Dr Hazel Butler takes 76 nursery rhymes and traditional community songs (*Odd Songs*) and explains the fascinating history and message behind them. Then, retaining the same rhythm and rhyming, she converts them into *God Songs,* which tell the history and message of the Bible from Genesis to Revelation.

- Fun
- Witty
- Profound
- Instructive
- Educational

An ideal gift!

"a stunning and unusual book...delightful and totally compelling, which forced me to think right out of my box. I laughed all the way through, but it often made me think at an uncomfortably deep level...utterly refreshing!"

Jen Rees Larcombe
Author and Speaker
Founder of the Charity *Beauty From Ashes*

Contact the author at info@whole-in-one.org.uk
for readings and speaking engagements

Fantastic resource for:

- Schools
- Families
- Outreach meetings
- Senior citizen groups
- All age worship

Hey Diddle Diddle!
I've cracked that old riddle
But now some others construe!
With wit, the odd laugh,
And 'Jesus thoughts',
It's my wish to convey them to you!

Order the book from www.whole-in-one.org.uk

£9.99

I KNOW A YOUNG WOMAN WHO SWALLOWED A LIE

God Songs from *Odd Songs*

By Dr Hazel Butler

In this unique and exciting new book, Dr Hazel Butler takes 76 nursery rhymes and traditional community songs (*Odd Songs*) and explains the fascinating history and message behind them. Then, retaining the same rhythm and rhyming, she converts them into *God Songs,* which tell the history and message of the Bible from Genesis to Revelation.

- Fun
- Witty
- Profound
- Instructive
- Educational

An ideal gift!

"a stunning and unusual book...delightful and totally compelling, which forced me to think right out of my box. I laughed all the way through, but it often made me think at an uncomfortably deep level...utterly refreshing!"

Jen Rees Larcombe
Author and Speaker
Founder of the Charity *Beauty From Ashes*

Contact the author at info@whole-in-one.org.uk for readings and speaking engagements

Fantastic resource for:

- Schools
- Families
- Outreach meetings
- Senior citizen groups
- All age worship

Hey Diddle Diddle!
I've cracked that old riddle
But now some others construe!
With wit, the odd laugh,
And 'Jesus thoughts',
It's my wish to convey them to you!

Order the book from www.whole-in-one.org.uk

£9.99

I Know a Young Woman who Swallowed a Lie

(*God Songs* from *Odd Songs*)

By Dr Hazel Butler

First published in 2010 by Onwards and Upwards
Publications, Berkeley House, 11 Nightingale Crescent,
West Horsley, Surrey, KT24 6PD

www.onwardsandupwardspublishing.com

ISBN: 978-1-907509-04-9

Cartoons by Robert Duncan www.duncancartoons.com

Cover design: Leah-Maarit

Printed in the UK

Further copies of this book are available from the author's website.

www.whole-in-one.org.uk

ABOUT THE AUTHOR

Hazel Butler, married to an Anglican clergyman for 41 years, was active in youth and family work within the parishes. She has 3 married sons and 10 grandchildren, and was a General Medical Practitioner for 30 years before she 'retired' in 2007. She has written a previous children's book *Heaven's Humpties* - a pre-cursor of this more adult and developed collection of *God Songs from Odd Songs*. She enjoys sharing her story and her rhymes with church and outreach groups.

She is on the board of International Health Partners, a charity dedicated to providing donated medical aid to the neediest parts of the world.

From her home in Tenterden, Kent, she runs prayer days and quiet days hoping to communicate the love of God in an up to date, relaxed and relevant way, especially to those who have no links to formal Christianity. More details are on *www.whole-in-one.org.uk*.

ACKNOWLEDGEMENT

This book has cost me many sleepless nights as these tunes and lyrics churned endlessly round in my head! Imagine the guilt I feel at imposing this suffering onto my good friend Abegail Morley! She acknowledges that it nearly drove her mad!

Nevertheless, disregarding the accompanying insomnia, and despite having climbed the dizzy heights of being short listed for the prestigious *Forward Prize for the Best First Collection of Poetry* she faithfully scanned this manuscript for errors! She was kept very busy, and I am hugely grateful to her for her nit-picking perfectionism! Perhaps she found in my book the answer to her collection of poems *How to Pour Madness into a Teacup!*

She has been a loyal friend, encouraging me throughout the formation of this book, steering me through the maze of possible publishing options, and persuading me that there may be other people 'out there' who would have the same quirky sense of humour as I have, as well as a delight in the amazing message of the Bible! I hope she's right!

Thank you, Abi!

FOREWORD

Jesus was a superb storyteller. Some of the stories He made up and some He adapted. There's no doubt that even little children listened to Him. There is no hint in the Gospels that any of the disciples were directed to take the little ones into a side room for a kind of Sunday school! The children found Jesus as easy to listen to as the grown-ups because everyone loves a story. He spoke of a lost child, a lost sheep and a lost piece of silver; He talked of good seed and poor seed, seed that dried up and seed that was crowded out by weeds; He referred to treasure hidden in a field and a pearl of great price. The Bible says "*the common people heard Him gladly*". They all, young and old, related to those stories, and they remembered them easily, ruminated over them and doubtless retold them.

This book is full of stories and a source of information, which must have included hours of hard work in research.

Here is a vast world of original imagination, which will inspire children's teachers and intrigue their parents.

This is a treasure of sermonettes which will enable children to capture something of the eternal truths of the Kingdom of God – of Jesus and 'His story'.

I congratulate Hazel for all her patience and skill in putting this resource together and pray that it will accomplish something of the evangelistic vision which inspired it.

David Pytches
Author and International Speaker
Previously Bishop in South America
Past Rector of St Andrew's Church, Chorleywood

PREFACE

Have you ever wondered where nursery rhymes came from? Why have generations of children sung them on their mothers' knees, learnt them at school, played them in the playground and remembered them to their dying days? Do you even understand them? Some of them are so weird that they seem to make no sense at all! How can you grow silver bells in a garden, and what exactly are 'cockle shells'? How can a woman live in a shoe or twenty-four blackbirds be baked in a pie? And so the questions go on, and yet, somehow, these strange rhymes and songs have become part of our British heritage! They tell something of the story of our nation.

Many date back to the Middle Ages and have been added to over the years, reflecting the customs and culture of their time. Some just started as family favourites – fun songs, games, or lullabies. Many would have been educational – teaching children to count, to read or to understand the right way to behave. But most were never intended for the nursery, or even written for children. In the days before the printed press, they were a means of spreading news, and political and social gossip. They were often used to stir up unrest and discontent amongst the lower classes, and some even held the seeds of rebellion!

Their musical rhythms and easy rhyming made them 'stick', and repetition in the nursery perpetuated them for generations, until they became part of the whole nation's repertoire.

And so, over the centuries there has evolved this mish-mash of 'odd songs' and stories that are deeply embedded in our culture. They contribute to our understanding of our history, our family and social life, and help us to understand where we, as English speaking people, came from, and the influences that have made us what we are.

We are not the only nation that has gathered up important stories and experiences and passed them on to succeeding generations. The Jewish race also has its collection of stories, songs, and teachings. At first they were part of the Jewish heritage, and were later embraced by all those who follow Yahweh – the God worshipped initially by the Jewish race and later followed by all Christians.

This collection of stories is known today as *The Old* and *The New Testament*. The first was the story of the Jews, and the second of the Christians who believed that Jesus was the Special One from God (The Messiah), who was promised in the Old Testament. The two books together form the Bible. It was written by about 50 authors, over a period of about 1500 years, and, like our nursery rhymes, includes history, moral direction, education, and songs of joy and hope. It teaches about family, social and political life. It describes how the Jewish race came into being, and how the Christian faith developed from it. Above all, it is revolutionary! The whole way through there runs a message that was geared to turn the world upside down! Sometimes the message is hidden and difficult to understand, and at other times it screams out, loud and clear, "God will rescue the poor, the disadvantaged, the marginalised, the sick, the abandoned, and sinners! God has intervened! Change has happened! Victory has been won!"

Despite the disparate nature of the Biblical writings, there is one central, clear focus – Jesus Christ, and the way He brought God's Kingdom to earth. The Old Testament points forward to His coming. The Gospels recount His arrival, His message, His ministry, and His death and resurrection. The rest of the New Testament tells of the formation of the early church, and the spread of the Good News, and looks forward to Jesus' coming again at the end of time, as we know it.

So, recognising that it is the simplicity, the catchy rhythms and easy rhyming of nursery rhymes that makes them stick in one's mind, I have taken 76 English *odd songs*, (nursery rhymes and community songs) and, retaining their form, rhythm and rhyming, have converted them into *God songs*. These tell the story of the history and teaching of the Jewish race and the Christian faith. Like nursery rhymes, they have a message for children and adults alike, and can be used from the cradle to the grave, collectively or individually, meditatively or jubilantly. They celebrate our amazing Christian heritage, centred on the life, death and resurrection of Jesus Christ, God's unique Son.

INTRODUCTION

In this collection, the traditional *odd song* is written on the left hand page and is followed by a brief summary of its known or speculated history. Many of the original texts are lost or distorted, but here I have reproduced what I consider to be the most likely, most imaginative or the most interesting history of the rhymes! Some have just evolved, or been created by fertile minds, but others will surprise you that such apparently innocent children's rhymes could have such gruesome or malevolent origins!

God songs, like the *odd songs*, are steeped in history. There is usually some link, (even if somewhat tenuous!) between the content of the *odd song* and the equivalent *God song*, which is written on the right hand page. Each *God song* is accompanied by a summary of its content and its context within the Bible, and by the relevant Biblical references.

The *God songs* are set out in sequence, taking us step by step through the Bible. The first few describe the formation and history of the Israelite nation, the failures and successes of Israel's leaders, and the clarion call of the men called 'prophets', urging the people to follow God's laws. The next few look at some of Israel's national songs (the Psalms), expressing the writer's fear, joy, despair and hope.

God songs then deal with the birth, teaching and death of the pivotal figure, Jesus, celebrating the extraordinary nature of His arrival, and the political intrigue that surrounded it. Just as some of the *odd songs* are revolutionary, expressing the discontent and suffering of the disadvantaged, so the message of Jesus was revolutionary. He turned the world and its values upside down. He taught that the poor were loved and accepted by God and that the 'failures' of the world could be forgiven, and given a new start. *God songs* look at the circumstances of Jesus' death, and resurrection, which heralded a new start, a new hope, and new life for His followers. They look at the subsequent formation of the Christian community, the life style and teaching of these 'Christ-ones', the persecution they suffered, and their hope of the return of Jesus in glory.

So we embark on this celebration of the history and heritage of two peoples - the people of Britain, and the people of God. Have fun and enjoy!

INDEX

First Line of *Odd Song*	First Line of *God Song*	Biblical Subject of *God Song*
JESUS' BIRTH		
19. Hark, Hark the Dogs do Bark	Hark, Hark how Angels Mark	The announcement of Jesus' birth by the angels
20. Little Boy Blue	Listen it's True	Jesus' birth
21. Christmas is Coming	Christmas is Coming	Jesus comes to earth
22. Little Jack Horner	Little Jack Horner	God's love in Jesus
THE WISE MEN FOLLOW THE STAR		
23. Twinkle Twinkle	Twinkle Twinkle	The wise men and the star
THE MASSACRE OF INFANTS UNDER TWO		
24. Cobbler Cobbler Mend my Shoe	Toddler Toddler Under Two	Jesus' first two years
JESUS' TEACHING		
25. Hey Diddle Diddle	Hey Diddle Diddle	The Scriptures are fulfilled in Jesus
26. See Saw Marjory Daw	See Saw Marjory Daw	One cannot serve God and money
27. It's raining It's Pouring	It's Raining It's Pouring	Watch and pray
28. Three Blind Mice	Three Blind Guys	Jesus - The Light of the world
29. Little Tommy Tucker	Little Tommy Tucker	God gives good gifts to His children
30. Hark, Hark	Hark, Hark	God cares for us
31. One Man Went to Mow	One Man Went to Sow	We must tell everyone the Good News
STORIES JESUS TOLD		
32. Hickory Dickory Dock	Hickory Dickory Dock	Life as a Race The houses built on sand and rock The sheep and the goats Jesus stands at the door and knocks
33. Three Little Kittens	One Loving Daddy	The Prodigal son
34. Old King Cole	Old King Cole	The King's wedding feast
35. Doctor Foster	Lady Lost a	The lost coins

First Line of *Odd Song*	First Line of *God Song*	Biblical Subject of *God Song*
36. Jack be Nimble	Jack was Simple	We must let our light shine
37. Mary, Mary Quite Contrary	Mary, Mary Quite Contrary	The Sower
38. Baa Baa Black Sheep	Baa Baa Black Sheep	The Good Shepherd
39. Mary had a Little Lamb	Jesus had a Little Lamb	The Good Shepherd
40. Little Bo Peep	Jesus did Weep	The Good Shepherd

PEOPLE JESUS MET AND
MIRACLES THAT HE
PERFORMED

41. Ding Dong Bell	Ding Dong Bell	The Samaritan woman at the well
42. There was an Old Woman	There was a Rich Ruler	The rich young ruler
43. Miss Polly had a Dolly	Miss Jairus had a Virus	The healing of Jairus's daughter
44. Peter, Peter Pumpkin Eater	Peter, Peter Challenge Greeter	Peter walks on water
45. Row, Row, Row your Boat	Row, Row, Row your Boat	Jesus calms the storm
46. Oh! Pussy Cat, Pussy Cat	So Busy that, Busy that	Martha and Mary

JESUS' DEATH AND
RESURRECTION

47. Ride a Cock Horse	Ride a Colt Horse	Christ's entry into Jerusalem
48. Pat-a-cake	Bread of Life	The last supper
49. Round and Round the Garden	Round and Round the Garden	Jesus in Gethsemane
50. Jack and Jill	Jack and Jill	Jesus' trial and crucifixion
51. The Queen of Hearts	The King of Hearts	Jesus' victory over Satan
52. This Old Man	Our Great God	The resurrection appearances

JESUS' GOOD NEWS

53. Humpty Dumpty	Humpty Dumpty	Jesus mends broken people
54. Oh! The Grand Old Duke of York	Oh! Our Mighty God in Heav'n	The way to Heaven
55. Hot Cross Buns	Hot Cross Buns	Our sins are forgiven
56. Rub a Dub Dub	Rub a Dub Dub	All are welcome to God's family
57. Simple Simon	Troubled Triston	Salvation is a free gift

First Line of *Odd Song*	First Line of *God Song*	Biblical Subject of *God Song*
THE EARLY CHURCH (THE ACTS OF THE APOSTLES)		
59. Tom, Tom the Piper's Son	Paul, Paul a Jewish Son	Paul is persecuted
60. Two Little Dicky Birds	Two Willing Missionaries	Peter and Paul
61. This Little Piggy	This Little Christian	The church shares all their possessions
THE LETTERS WRITTEN BY THE APOSTLES		
62. Oh Dear! What Can the Matter be?	Oh Dear! What Can the Matter be?	All things work together for good (Romans)
63. Half a Pound of Tuppenny Rice	Have you Found You Try to be Nice?	The struggle between good and evil (Romans)
64. If You're Happy and You Know it	If You're Happy and You Know it	We must share the good news (Romans)
65. Jack Sprat	Fleet Feet	We are all parts of one body (1 Corinthians)
66. Little Miss Muffet	Little Miss Muffet	The power of Scripture (Ephesians)
67. Itsy Bitsy Spider	It's This Bit of Pride Here	The need to be humble (Philippians)
68. Rock a Bye Baby	Rock the Christ Baby	Jesus' victory over Hell
69. Polly Put the Kettle On	Polly Get the Bible Out	We should read the Scriptures
70. Diddle Diddle Dumpling	Tittle Tattle Grumbling	The power of the tongue
71. Goosey Goosey Gander	Who's He Who Meanders?	Discerning the truth (Jude)
72. Peter Piper	'Postle Peter	Peter's epistles (1 Peter)
73. Daisy, Daisy	Praise Him, Praise Him	We should give glory to God (Jude)
THE VISION OF JOHN AS DESCRIBED IN REVELATIONS		
74. Pease Porridge Hot	Some Churches Hot	The letters to the churches
75. Oranges and Lemons	How is it Love Left Us?	The letters to the churches
JESUS SECOND COMING		
76. She'll be Coming Round the Mountain	He will Come to Olive Mountain	Jesus' second coming

11

1

Georgie Porgie, puddin' and pie,

Kissed the girls and made them cry;

When the boys came out to play

Georgie Porgie ran away.

This rhyme is thought to have originated from the Stuart era. *Georgie Porgie* was the nickname given to George Villiers, who lived from 1592 – 1628. He was the First Duke of Buckingham, and was a courtier in the reign of King James I. He had a very close relationship with the King, and was also known to be a notorious 'ladies' man'. Amongst his many affairs was a liaison with Anne of Austria, the Queen of France. His fickleness broke many women's hearts. This, together with his unwelcome influence over the King, led Parliament to lose patience with him and ban James from intervening on his behalf and protecting him.

George Villier's lifestyle was the result of man defying God and going his own way. Self-centredness is the natural condition of every one of us since Adam and Eve first rebelled against God. This initial parody explains that all the stories told in this book demonstrate that the relationship between God and man was destroyed by man's sin. It broke God's heart because He knew that the result of this should be death and separation of man from God. (The Gospels tell us that 'Jesus wept' when He saw the sin of Jerusalem.) But God loved the world so much that He planned its rescue by sending Jesus, His only Son. Jesus describes Himself as *'The Way'* to God. The fall of mankind, and God's plan of rescue, is the core message of the Bible, and therefore the core message of this book.

1A

All these stories couldn't deny

This, God's world, has made Him cry.

Sin destroys, but shout, 'Hurray!'

For the Lord, has planned *'The Way'!*

Romans 3 v 19 - 20

Romans 6 v 23

John 3 v 16

John 14 v 6

2

The wheels of the bus go round and round,

Round and round, round and round;

The wheels of the bus go round and round,

All day long.

This is a modern children's song with lots of actions throughout different verses. Its origin is unknown, but it encourages group participation and imagination and will give future generations a good insight into one of our modes of transport!

Sometimes we may feel that the earth just goes round and round, like the wheels of the bus - always has done, and always will! But this next *God song* takes us back to the very beginning when God made the world and everything in it, from nothing.

First, He brought light into the world, and divided night from day. He then separated the sky from the waters underneath it, and made sea and dry land.

Next He made all the different plants, followed by the sun, moon and stars. Eventually He filled the earth and the sea with all the animals, from creepy crawlies, to huge monsters.

The final expression of his creativity, the pinnacle of it all, was man and woman. He made them with His own image stamped on them, and able to relate to him, in a loving and cooperative way. God was delighted with His work, and, after these six phases of creation, He stopped and admired His handiwork, and set out to enjoy it!

Genesis 1, 2

The wheel of the earth goes round and round,
Round and round, round and round;
The wheel of the earth goes round and round,
All day long.

For God made the light and called it day,
Called it day, called it day;
The morn and the eve were made that way,
On day one.

And God split the waters – made the sky,
Made the sky, made the sky;
With water below and some up high,
On day two.

And God caused the land to grow some plants,
Grow some plants, grow some plants;
For none of them got there just by chance,
On day three.

And God made the sun, the stars and moon,
Stars and moon, stars and moon;
The sky brightened up with lights all strewn,
On day four.

And God made the fish and birds that fly,
Birds that fly, birds that fly;
The fish filled the sea, and birds the sky,
On day five.

And God made the beasts both large and small,
Large and small, large and small;
He then made a man to rule them all,
On day six.

And God looked around and liked His work,
Liked His work, liked his work;
He took the day off – deserved this perk,
On day seven.

The tale we have told you may astound,
May astound, may astound,
But this is the truth that's so profound,
God made all!

3

I know an old woman who swallowed a fly

This song is just fun and ridiculous as it describes the bizarre eating habits of an old woman, followed by the words, 'She died, of course!" We all die, of course! But why? Where did death come from?

After God had made the perfect world, an evil spirit called Satan wanted to break God's supreme authority, and was hell bent (literally!) on persuading man to assert his independence. So, in the form of a snake, he tempted Eve to eat the fruit from a very special tree that God had forbidden her to touch. Eve thought the fruit looked too good to resist and decided to disobey God, and eat it. She persuaded Adam to do the same.

Adam and Eve's disobedience destroyed the perfect relationship they had with God. Everything God had warned them about happened. They became riddled with guilt, they felt distanced from God, and sin, suffering and death were introduced into the world.

This situation has continued ever since, with mankind trying to assert his independence from God, and to make his way without Him. But God's love never wavered and He pursued mankind passionately. Eventually He bridged that gap created by man, by coming into the world to re-establish the love relationship that He once had with Adam and Eve. To do this He had to die, and win the battle over sin and death – but more of that anon!

This *God song* describes the sequence of events that led to death entering the world, and how God eventually defeated it.

Genesis 3

I know an old woman who swallowed a fly;
I don't know why she swallowed a fly.
Perhaps she'll die.

I know an old woman who swallowed a spider
That wriggled and jiggled and tickled inside her.
She swallowed a spider to catch the fly;
I don't know why she swallowed a fly.
Perhaps she'll die.

I know an old woman who swallowed a bird.
How absurd to swallow a bird!
She swallowed the bird to catch the spider
That wriggled and jiggled and tickled inside her.
She swallowed the spider to catch the fly;
I don't know why she swallowed a fly.
Perhaps she'll die.

I know a young woman, who swallowed a lie;
I don't know why Eve swallowed this lie,
"You will not die!"

I know the old serpent who followed beside her,
Who wriggled and niggled; the truth he denied her.
He followed beside her, this catch to try,
"Your God defy!" She swallowed this lie;
"You will not die!"

I know that young woman just followed his word.
How absurd to follow his word!
She followed the word of the snake beside her
Who wriggled and niggled; the truth he denied her.
He followed beside her, this catch to try,
'"Your God defy!" She swallowed this lie,
"You will not die!"

I know an old woman who swallowed a cat;
Imagine that! She swallowed a cat.
She swallowed the cat to catch the bird;
She swallowed the bird to catch the spider
That wriggled and jiggled and tickled inside her.
She swallowed the spider to catch the fly;
I don't know why she swallowed a fly.
Perhaps she'll die.

I know an old woman who swallowed a dog.
What a hog, to swallow a dog!
She swallowed the dog to catch the cat;
She swallowed the cat to catch the bird;
She swallowed the bird to catch the spider
That wriggled and jiggled and tickled inside her!
She swallowed the spider to catch the fly;
I don't know why she swallowed a fly.
Perhaps she'll die.

I know that old Adam just swallowed her chat;
Imagine that! He swallowed her chat!
He swallowed her chat, believed her word,
And followed the word of the snake beside her
Who wriggled and niggled; the truth he denied her.
He followed beside her, this catch to try,
"Your God defy!" She swallowed this lie,
"You will not die!"

I know in the garden she's followed by God.
Wasn't that odd! She's followed by God!
She's followed by God who came to chat;
He's sorrowing that they'd heard the word;
Yes, followed the word the snake beside her,
Who wriggled and niggled; the truth he denied her.
He followed beside her, this catch to try,
"Your God defy!" She swallowed this lie,
"You will not die!"

...INNOCENT...

I know an old woman who swallowed a goat;
Opened her throat, and down went the goat!
She swallowed the goat to catch the dog;
She swallowed the dog to catch the cat;
She swallowed the cat to catch the bird;
She swallowed the bird to catch the spider
That wriggled and jiggled and tickled inside her;
She swallowed the spider to catch the fly;
I don't know why she swallowed a fly;
Perhaps she'll die!

I know an old woman who swallowed a cow;
I don't know how she swallowed a cow;
She swallowed the cow to catch the goat;
She swallowed the goat to catch the dog;
She swallowed the dog to catch the cat;
She swallowed the cat to catch the bird;
She swallowed the bird to catch the spider
That wriggled and jiggled and tickled inside her;
She swallowed the spider to catch the fly;
I don't know why she swallowed a fly;
Perhaps she'll die.

I know an old woman who swallowed a horse;
She died of course!

I know they were naked; with horror they note
They had no coat, with horror they note!
With horror they vote to hide from God,
When followed by God who came to chat;
He's sorrowing that she'd heard the word,
Yes, followed the word of the snake beside her;
Who wriggled and niggled; the truth he denied her.
He followed beside her, this catch to try,
"Your God defy!" She swallowed this lie,
"You will not die!"

I know that this lie it still follows us now;
Oh, just see how it follows us now!
It follows us now; St Paul he wrote,
We've wandered, he wrote, so far from God.
Still followed by God, who longs to chat;
Who, longing to chat, has sent his Word;
Let's follow the Word, who lived beside us,
And signalled new life, with His Spirit inside us.
Let's swallow our pride and forget that lie;
We'll not defy the Lord God on high;
Then we won't die!

I know that to save us, Christ suffered the cross;
He rose of course!

4

Ten green bottles hanging on the wall;

Ten green bottles hanging on the wall;

And if one green bottle should accidentally fall,

There'd be nine green bottles hanging on the wall.

Nine green bottles hanging on the wall……..etc

In September 1998, a French scholar, Pierre d'Ouidlede discovered a page of manuscript, apparently dating from the late 14th century, containing what seems to be an early version of this song, in Chaucerian English! Could Chaucer's pilgrims have sung it to pass the time of day?

Another possibility is that it originated in the 1820s when Sir Robert Peel's metropolitan police were known as 'greenbottles' because of their green uniforms. What could be more satisfying to local criminals than seeing those responsible for hanging them fall, one by one?

4A

Ten good people, hang your hopes on all;
Ten good people, hang your hopes on all;
For if these good people should act amiss and fall,
There'd be no good people and no hope at all.

Adam *toppled* when he followed Eve;
Ate the *apple* he was told to leave;
When the snake talked *twaddle*, he actually believed;
That leaves nine good people having to achieve.

(Genesis 2 - 3)

Noah *got all* ready for the flood;
Had some *bottle*, built an ark of wood;
Then he got so *sozzled,* he lay there in the nude;
That leaves eight good people. Can they all stay good?

(Genesis 6 - 9)

Jonah *bottled* out of Nineveh;
Chose to *stop all* plans and so defer;
Said, "This passing *yacht'll* go where I would prefer!"
That leaves seven good people. Can they fail to err?

(Jonah 1 - 4)

Abram *wobbled,* having had the thought,

This is *what I'll* do if Sarah's sought!

Though I tied the *knot I'll* say, "That's my <u>sis</u> I brought!"

That leaves six good people – acting as they ought?

(Genesis 12 v 1 – 9, Genesis 20)

Isaac *spotted* jealousy was rife.

So he *cobbled* tails to save his life;

Got it in his *noddle* to swear he had no wife;

That leaves five good people. Can it stay at five?

(Genesis 26 v 7 – 11)

Jacob *squabbled,* had a dreadful fight;

Stirred up *trouble,* stealing Esau's right;

And he said, "Old *pop'll* not see –he's lost his sight!"

That leaves four good people. Can they act aright?

(Genesis 27)

Joseph *modelled* rainbow coats – looked swell!

As a *toddler,* futures could foretell!

And by dad so *coddled,* he gave his brothers hell!

That leaves three good people. Can they turn out well?

(Genesis 37)

Just as the ten green bottles fall down one by one, so do humans, and have done so since the beginning of time. Once Adam and Eve had disobeyed God, the world was never the same again. Somehow man's very nature was distorted, and he found it impossible to live as God had initially intended. Some were more successful than others, and this next parody tells of some of the best men we read about in the Old Testament, but even they failed.

Noah got drunk, to his sons' acute embarrassment.

Jonah disobeyed God, and ran away rather than warn the people of Nineveh of God's impending judgement.

Abram was scared that the king would want his wife, so pretended she was his sister.

Isaac thought the local young men might fancy his wife, so, like his dad, pretended she was his sister.

Jacob tricked his brother out of his blessing.

Joseph was spoilt by his dad, who gave him a rainbow coloured coat. He dreamt his brothers would eventually bow down to him – and told them so, much to their fury!

Moses lost his cool with the Children of Israel when they kept on moaning.

David killed Uriah in order to get his wife!

Not a huge list of success!

There has only ever been one person who lived a perfect life. That was Jesus, God's Son. Oh yes! He was tempted to disobey God. He fought against Satan all His life, but He never gave in. He came into the world to show us how a perfect life should be lived. Not only that, He also took on to Himself all the mess mankind had made of their lives and their relationship with God and with each other, and sacrificed everything to put it right once again.

Moses *bottled* anger well at first;

Then he *got all* angry and he cursed;

And he could have *throttled* all those who moaned of thirst;

That leaves two good people. Can we know their worst?

(Numbers 11 v10 – 1, 20 v 1 - 13)

Should we *model* on King David's life?

No! He *ogled* at Uriah's wife;

When he killed and *got all* he wanted, - oh what strife!

That leaves one good person. Can this one survive?

(2 Samuel 11)

Jesus *struggled*, bore the guilt of all;

Though He *took all* sin, He didn't fall;

And He doesn't *bottle* our wrongs, nor them re-call;

But forgives bad people, whom He'll re-install.

Romans 5 v 12 - 21

Isaiah 43 v 25

Micah 7 v 18 – 20

5

Old MacDonald had a farm;
Ee-i, ee-i-o!
And on that farm he had a cow;
Ee-i, ee-i-o!
With a moo-moo! Here,
And a moo-moo! There;
Here a moo! There a moo!
Everywhere a moo-moo!
Old MacDonald had a farm.
Ee-i, ee-i-o!

Old MacDonald had a farm;
Ee-i, ee-i-o!
And on that farm
He had a horse;
Ee-i, ee-i-o!
With a neigh-neigh! Here,
And a neigh-neigh! There;
Here a neigh! There a neigh!
Everywhere a neigh-neigh!

With a moo-moo! Here,
And a moo-moo! There;
Here a moo! There a moo!
Everywhere a moo-moo!

Old MacDonald had a farm.
Ee-i, ee-i-o!

First Group	Second Group
<u>First Group</u>	<u>Second Group</u>
Old man Noah built an ark,	God saw Noah – picked him out;
Ee-i, ee-i-o!	Ee-i, ee-i-o!
But all his mates thought it a lark;	For he alone was still devout;
Ee-i, ee-i-o!	Ee-i, ee-i-o!
With a Ha! Ha! Here,	With a prayer, prayer here,
And a Ha! Ha! There;	And a prayer, prayer there;
Here a Ha! There a Ha!	Here a prayer! There a prayer!
Everywhere a Ha! Ha!	Everywhere a prayer, prayer!
Old man Noah built an ark.	God saw Noah – picked him out.
Ee-i, ee-i-o!	Ee-i, ee-i-o!
God saw man defied His law;	God told Noah, "Build an ark!"
Ee-i, ee-i-o!	Ee-i, ee-i-o!
His wicked ways	"Pair all beasts
Grew more and more;	And then embark!"
Ee-i, ee-i-o!	Ee-i, ee-i-o!
With a ME! ME! Here,	With a … … (animal noise)! Here,
And a ME! ME! There;	And a … … There;
Here a ME! There a ME!	Here a … ! There a … !
Everywhere it's ME! ME!	Everywhere a … … !
With a Ha! Ha! Here,	With a prayer, prayer! Here!
And a Ha! Ha! There,	And a prayer, prayer! There!
Here a Ha! There a Ha!	Here a prayer! There a prayer!
Everywhere a Ha! Ha!	Everywhere a prayer, prayer!
God saw man defied his law.	God told Noah, "Build an ark!"
Ee-i, ee-i-o!	Ee-i, ee-i-o!

Old MacDonald managed to gather together lots of animals, but nowhere near as many as Noah, who is the subject of our next *God song* and continues the story of man's rebellion against God. The world had got into a terrible state, and God was hugely angry and sad at how man had spoilt everything He had made. As He looked at the mess, God regretted having made man and He decided to destroy everything and start again. He would send a flood that would devastate the whole of the earth.

However, there was one man, Noah, who tried very hard to obey God despite the odds stacked against him. God loved Noah, and wanted to save him, so He decided to get him to build a great big boat (an ark), and use that to save himself and his family, and one pair of every animal that God had created. These would be the building blocks for a new start.

God declared He'd send a flood;

Ee-i, ee-i-o!

He'd drown the world

In sea and mud;

Ee-i, ee-i-o!

With a Split, Splat! Here,

And a Split Splat! There;

Here a Split! There a Splat!

Everywhere a Split, Splat!

And a ME! ME! Here,

And a ME! ME! There;

Here a ME! There a ME!

Everywhere it's ME! ME!

And a Ha! Ha! Here,

And a Ha! Ha! There;

Here a Ha! There a Ha!

Everywhere a Ha! Ha!

God declared He'd send a flood,

Ee-i, ee-i-o!

Old man Noah's safe and sound,

Ee-i, ee-i-o!

The floods have stopped,

They've hit the ground;

Ee-i, ee-i-o!

With a "Thank God!" Here,

And a "Thank God!" There;

Here a "Thanks!" There a "Thanks!"

Everywhere a "Thanks! Thanks!"

And a prayer, prayer! Here,

And a prayer, prayer! There;

Here a prayer! There a prayer!

Everywhere a prayer, prayer!

With a ... ... ! Here,

And a ... ... ! There;

Here a ... ! There a ... !

Everywhere a ... ...!

Old man Noah's safe and sound,

Ee-i, ee-i-o!

<u>Both Groups Together</u>

Let us praise our God right now;

Ee-i, ee-i-o!

To serve and follow Him let's vow;

Ee-i, ee-i-o!

So let's praise Him here!

And let's praise Him there!

Here a praise! There a praise!

Everywhere a praise, praise!

Let us praise our God right now.

Ee-i, ee-i-o!

Genesis 6 – 8

6

Rain! Rain! Go away!

Come again another day.

Little Johnny wants to play.

Rain, rain, go to Spain!

Never show your face again.

These words are said to date back to the reign of Queen Elizabeth I (1533-1603). The Spanish Armada invaded England in 1588 with 130 ships. To cope with this formidable force, the whole British navy could muster only thirty-six vessels, all much smaller than the largest of the Spanish ships. But merchants and private gentlemen fitted out vessels at their own expense, and by midsummer a fleet of one hundred and ninety-seven ships was placed at the disposal of the British admiral. The English managed to defeat the Armada – only 65 Spanish vessels returning home. It was thought that the English gained advantage by having very small ships that could manoeuvre swiftly, and by the dreadful stormy weather that scattered the Armada fleet. Hence this little nursery ditty!

The Spaniards were not the only ones to want the rain to go away. After Noah had got into the ark it rained for forty days and forty nights, and the whole earth was flooded. The only survivors of this phenomenal flood were Noah, his family and all the animals with him in the ark. Eventually the rain stopped, the waters receded, and the ark came to a standstill on top of a mountain. When Noah disembarked, he saw a wonderful rainbow in the sky. God told him that this was a special sign to mankind that He, God, would never flood the earth again in this way. He promised that the cycle of day and night, and crop sowing and harvesting would continue uninterrupted, and that the rainbow would remind people of this promise.

6A

Rain! Rain! Go away!

Noah's ark has come to stay.

See the rainbow on display!

Rain, rain, God makes plain,

He'll not flood this place again!

Genesis 9 v 8 – 17

7

Daisy, Daisy,

Give me your answer do!

I'm half crazy, all for the love of you.

It won't be a stylish marriage;

I can't afford a carriage;

But you'll look sweet upon the seat

Of a bicycle made for two!

Daisy, Daisy was composed by Harry Dacre in 1892 after he went to the United States with a bicycle, on which he had to pay duty. His friend, William Jerome, remarked lightly, "It's lucky you didn't bring a bicycle made for two, otherwise you'd have to pay double duty." Dacre was so taken with the phrase 'bicycle made for two' that he wrote this song.

The Daisy who inspired the song is thought to be the Countess of Warwick, Frances Evelyn Maynard. She was one of the wealthiest and most desirable English women of the period, and was, at one point, the mistress of the Prince of Wales (subsequently King Edward VII).

Daisy, Daisy is all about love, and love needs communication and communication usually needs words and a common language! This next *God song* tells again of the disastrous consequences of sin, and how it led to severe communication problems!

Humans had multiplied and spread all over the earth, but had forgotten that they were God's subjects. Some became proud and anxious for power, and decided to build a huge tower called Babel, which would represent man's power and dominion. This angered God, who decided to stop man in his proud tracks by confusing his language, so that communication between nations became difficult.

7A

Gaze, oh gaze at

Babel – 'The Tower with View!'

Now it's raised, we'll all of the world subdue!

But God, He decried this language,

Confused the tongues of man, which

Means, when you meet, it's hard to greet

Someone nice who's from Timbuktu!

Genesis 11

8

Cry baby bunting

Daddy's gone a-hunting;

Gone to fetch a rabbit skin

To wrap the baby bunting in.

These words would often be sung softly to a young child as a lullaby, or to explain the disappearance of father to a crying child! The earliest traceable publication is from 1784.

The baby in *Cry Baby Bunting* was crying because his daddy had gone away hunting - but the Bible tells us of another person who was very upset when someone went hunting. This next song tells us why.

As the human race grew, God decided to choose one man, Abraham, with whom He would develop a special relationship, and from whom would come a nation that would belong to God in a unique way. Abraham had a son called Isaac, who in turn had two sons, twins, called Esau and Jacob. Sibling rivalry ruled!

Jacob, the younger twin twice tricked his brother out of his inheritance rights. This song describes the way he, at his mother's suggestion, fooled his aged, blind father Isaac into giving him, instead of Esau, the first-born's special blessing. While Esau hunted for game to celebrate the blessing he was to receive, Jacob stayed at home and moped! Rebekah, his mother, hatched a plan, however. She cooked Isaac his favourite goat stew, and then covered Jacob's smooth skin with goat skin, to make him feel like his hairy brother. Jacob put on Esau's clothes and served the meal to his father, claiming that he was Esau, the elder son. Isaac was taken in by this trick, and gave the special blessing to Jacob - to Esau's absolute fury! Esau vowed to hunt Jacob down and take revenge.

8A

Why waves the bunting?
Happy Esau's hunting!
Game he'll catch, and drag it in,
To cap today - dad's blessing him!

Why's Jacob grumbling?
Sad his hopes are crumbling.
Scorns the wretched habit then
For Dads to favour older twin.

While Jacob's mumbling
Mummy's up to something.
Gone to sketch a plan for him;
So, p'raps today this son will win!

Sly lady's gloating;
Jacob's got a goat in!
"Come! We'll stretch its shaggy skin
To wrap your hairless body in."

"I've made a dumpling!
Daddy's tummy's rumbling!
Goat stew - fetch, and take it in.
Tell dad, I've made it just for him!"

Blind Isaac's fumbling!
"That's which son?" he's wond'ring.
"Son! Outstretch! – 'Tis Esau's skin!"
So, trapped, he prays, "Become King-pin!"

"Fie daddy's blundering!"
Angry Esau's thundering,
"Rotten, wretched, 'grab-it' twin!"
He snapped, "Today I'm done with him!"

Genesis 27

9

The bear went over the mountain,
The bear went over the mountain,
The bear went over the mountain
    To see what he could see.

And what d'you think he saw?

The other side of the mountain,
The other side of the mountain,
The other side of the mountain
    Was all that he could see.

God shared his law on the mountain,
God shared his law on the mountain,
God shared his law on the mountain;
   "Now see how man should be!"

While Moses got God's law

His brother sided with doubters,
His brother sided with doubters,
His brother sided with doubters;
   And all went on a spree!

Declared some gold, that was molten,
Declared some gold, that was molten,
Declared some gold, that was molten,
   To be their deity!

A golden calf was formed!

This, Moses spied from the mountain,
This, Moses spied from the mountain,
This, Moses spied from the mountain,
   Appalled by what he sees.

This is a favourite camp side song. It reminds me of a story in the Old Testament of some people who went over the mountain, but wandered around in circles, for forty years!

Jacob, (also known as Israel) had lots of children, who had lots of children, and so on, until his family had grown into a great nation – 'The Children of Israel'. They spent many years as slaves in Egypt until God appointed Moses to rescue them. He led them across the Red Sea, which was miraculously parted by God. God had promised He would lead them to a wonderful land of their own, but, because of their disobedience, God made them wander round the mountains for forty years before they eventually entered 'The Promised Land'.

At one stage God called Moses up to Mount Sinai and gave him the Ten Commandments - His special rules for how people should live. Meanwhile, the others at the bottom of the mountain were getting restless and bored. They began to doubt if Moses would ever come back, so decided to have a party! They melted down their gold jewellery and asked Aaron, Moses' brother, to make a god out of it that they could worship. This he did, and shaped it into the form of a calf.

Moses was furious when he saw what was going on and wondered if God could ever forgive them for such idolatry. He climbed back up the mountain and pleaded with God for mercy. In His amazing love, God forgave the Children of Israel and gave them another chance to obey Him and have that close relationship with Him restored

Then, bearing shame, he re-mounted,

Then, bearing shame, he re-mounted,

Then, bearing shame, he re-mounted,

For mercy was his plea.

And what d'you think he saw?

Another side of God's bounty,

Another side of God's bounty,

Another side of God's bounty,

For all who'd bow the knee!

Exodus 19 v 3

Exodus 32

Exodus 34 v 6

10

Bobby Shafto's gone to sea

With silver buckles on his knee;

When he comes back he'll marry me;

Oh! Bonny Bobby Shafto.

Robert Shafto, nicknamed 'Bonny Bobby Shafto', was born in 1732 in County Durham. He became MP for County Durham in 1760. This song is said to refer to the way he broke the heart of Bridget Belasyse of Brancepeth Castle, County Durham, who died two weeks after hearing the news that Bobby had married Anne Duncombe in Yorkshire.

I guess Bobby Shafto went to sea for adventure, intending to come back. But Jonah, in our next song, ran away to sea in order to escape from God. The thing was, God was very angry with the people of Nineveh who were wicked and rebellious. His justice demanded punishment, but His great love wanted to forgive.

This next song tells of how He sent Jonah to warn the Ninevites to repent and change. Jonah, however, thought that they deserved punishment, so he ran away to sea, in the opposite direction, to avoid having to warn them, and possibly see them repent and be forgiven! God stopped him by sending a storm that nearly shipwrecked him. It wasn't until Jonah admitted his disobedience, and the sailors threw him overboard, that the storm stopped. God organised for a great fish to swallow Jonah, and, three days later, to vomit him up on dry land, so that he had a second chance to obey God, and go to Nineveh.

Jonah had learnt a lot, but he still couldn't cope with God forgiving wicked people! 'Religious' people can still feel better than others, and think that 'really bad people' should not go unpunished! But thank Goodness (literally!), although we all deserve God's punishment, He offers forgiveness to all, because He bore the consequences of everyone's sin when He died on the cross. All we have to do is genuinely repent just as the people of Nineveh did.

Jonah 1 - 4

God, His heart so torn to see
How sin corrupted Nineveh,
Said, "I must sack this city, see
They've long from God departed."

So he drafted Jonah; he
Said, "I'll disrupt their revelries!
Just go, get packed, and carry these -
God's warnings of disaster."

Jonah 'passed' on this, for he
Could hold no truck with God if He,
When men changed tack, just set them free.
He'd not become their pastor!

So, departing angrily,
He'd pit his luck out there at sea.
He'd not stay back, nor tarry he,
To follow God's hard asking!

Pleasure craft 'twas not to be!
For God soon struck a storm at sea,
And proved the fact you cannot flee
From God, to dodge His task so!

NINEVEH

Then at last the crew agree
To kill the luckless boy, and see,
When they have jacked him in the sea,
If God's great wrath then passes.

One fish passed and thought with glee,
"Cor! This poor sucker's good for tea!"
But sicked him back on day '0 – 3';
And so the prophet started.

Preached his heart out, then could see
That they were touched by God's decree;
Their proud wills cracked, and on his knee
Each bowed to God and fasted.

Jonah parted company;
He'd had a hunch how it would be;
God has a knack of setting free
All those who'd stop and hearken.

Though it's past and history,
I'm still so struck how it will be!
For back on track He'll carry me,
Once God becomes my Master.

And so it is that we too can share this wonderful news that Jonah was to have passed to the Ninevites - that God forgives repentant sinners! Christ secured the victory over Satan when He rose from the dead, and one day He will come back and His victory will be complete. Then, those who have accepted His forgiveness will be accepted by God as though they had never sinned! No past scores to be settled!

10A *continued*

Come and laugh for soon we'll see
Old Satan buckle at the knee,
When Christ comes back in victory,
Our wrongs will not be charted!

11

I'm a little tea pot, short and stout.

Here's my handle, here's my spout!

When I see the tea cups hear me shout;

Tip me up and pour me out!

It is often assumed that this is an anonymous nursery rhyme written in Victorian England. However, it is claimed by Ronald Sanders that it was written by his father, George Harry Sanders, in New York in 1939 and was written for aspiring tap dance tots, who were too young to perform the usual dance manoeuvres. The song came to the public's notice when Horace Heidt, a bandleader, played it on the radio.

Sometimes we talk about being 'poured out' for God. This means allowing God to turn things upside down in your life, and giving everything to Him.

This next *God song* tells of such a man in the Old Testament, called Isaiah. In those days God chose certain very special people, called prophets, to pass His messages on to the wicked and disobedient people around them. Isaiah was a prophet, and was considered to be holy and devout, compared with those around him - until he met with God in the temple. That soon changed his perspective. His sin became all too obvious against the absolute purity and glory of God. He immediately fell down and cried out in despair, "It's all over! I am doomed!" But God sent angels to touch his unclean lips with burning coals, and he was forgiven. God then asked who would take His message to those who had not heard it. Isaiah's ready response was, "Here I am! Send me!"

I'm Isaiah – see, I'm called 'devout'!
Here's no scandal, there's no doubt!
Till I see God's glory, then I shout,
"I'm corrupt and flawed throughout!"

Though with guilt I'm seized, God sorts me out!
See His angels fly about.
Then I hear a "Get up!" – and a shout,
"Him we've touched is pure throughout!"

I'm forgiven! - See what 't's all about!
See God handle fears and doubt!
When I hear God's 'call-up', hear me shout,
"Pick me up! Send *your* man out!"

Isaiah 6 v 1 - 8

12

Goosey, goosey gander

Whither will you wander?

Upstairs, downstairs,

In my lady's chamber.

There I met an old man

Who wouldn't say his prayers.

I took him by the left leg

And threw him down the stairs.

This rhyme possibly dates back to the 16th century when Catholic priests had to hide in 'priest holes' (very small secret rooms, once found in many great houses in England) to avoid persecution from zealous Protestants. The 'goosey, goosey' refers to the goose step marching of Oliver Cromwell's army. The soldiers would often look 'upstairs and downstairs' in the hopes of catching some recalcitrant catholic priest. If caught, the priest would have a rope tied around his ankle and he would be hurled down the stairs until he confessed or died. A 'left leg' or 'left footer' became an abusive name for a Catholic. If the priest wouldn't say his prayers in English rather than Latin, he would be executed.

The next *God song* tells of the rivalry between two other religious factions - the faithful Israelites who worshipped Jehovah, and those who had shifted their allegiance to heathen gods. Many began to worship Baal, and Elijah, a prophet of Jehovah, challenged them to make up their minds and decide who the true God was. He taunted the prophets of Baal, challenging them to a competition. Each side would prepare an animal sacrifice, but instead of setting fire to it the prophets would ask their own god to send fire to consume it. Baal's prophets ranted and raved, but nothing happened. Elijah, on the other hand, soaked his animal in water, and then quietly asked Jehovah to reveal Himself in power. Immediately, flames of fire descended from Heaven, and the beast was consumed. The people realised once again that Jehovah was the true God, and worshipped Him without reservation.

12A

"You see! You meander!
Whither will you wander?
This way? That way?
Will you stray much longer?
I will meet with Baal's men
Who bully Baal with prayers.
I'll put them to the test then -
The true God - ours or theirs?

You'll see who is stronger,
Which God's a responder!
For Baal will fail,
Though they rave for longer!"
'Lija wet his old bull;
Jehovah heard his prayers.
He looked and with a deft hand
Consumed it with His flares.

1 Kings 18 v 21 - 39

13

Ladybird, ladybird

Fly away home!

Your house is on fire; your children are gone!

All except one and that's little Nan.

She had crept under the warming pan.

The word *ladybird* here has nothing to do with little red, spotted insects, but was a derivative of 'Our Lady', the Catholic name used for Mary, the mother of Jesus. The Act of Uniformity (1559 & 1662) forbade priests to hold Mass, so they held it secretly in the open fields. This rhyme may have been used as a warning to defiant priests. Attendants risked being thrown into jail, and the priests tortured, and then burnt alive at the stake, or hung, drawn and quartered. Guy Fawkes, who tried to blow up the Houses of Parliament, suffered in this fashion.

The sufferings alluded to in *Ladybird, Ladybird,* could well cause the victims to question where God is when things go wrong. Job, another prophet in the Old Testament, must have asked this question too, when he lost all his family, possessions and even his own health. He had served God loyally, and pleased Him in every way. As a result God initially blessed him, both materially and with good health, and he had a large successful family.

This annoyed Satan, and he decided to have a go at Job. He realised, however, that God was protecting him, and he wouldn't have a hope of tempting Job successfully unless God removed His protection. Satan challenged God to allow him to test Job to see if he would remain faithful even in the midst of tragedy and suffering.

Despite all sorts of trials and sickness sent by Satan, Job, although he could not understand why God appeared to have abandoned him, remained loyal to God, trusting Him, and believing that He still had everything in control.

Job 1 and 2 v 6 - 8

13A

Satan heard, Satan heard
Job did no wrong.
Of God he enquired, "But would he stay strong,
Still respect you and still be your man
If you kept mum? So! Withdraw your hand!

Say he heard, say he heard
He'd lost his home,
His farm was on fire; his children were gone?
Don't expect then he'd still be your fan!"
So he dreamt up an appalling plan.

Then occurred, then occurred
All Satan said.
From robbers and fire, Job's children were dead.
As he wept tears, his boils and sores ran,
Still he kept humble before all man.

Undeterred, undeterred,
Job knelt in prayer.
His suffering dire, yet still he declared,
"Why reject God? – He's not just a scam;
Why defect now from His Master Plan?

By his word, By His word,
God made us all,
And I will aspire to trust him for all;
None except God can know how t'will pan,
I accept humbly, He's Lord of man."

14

London Bridge is falling down,

Falling down, falling down,

London Bridge is falling down,

My fair lady.

The original London Bridge dates back to the Roman occupation of Britain in the 1st century and was made of wood and clay. Subsequent verses describe the various building materials that were used later to try to fortify the collapsing bridge. Viking invaders destroyed the bridge around 1014, and stronger materials were used after that, and a drawbridge constructed. The first stone bridge was built in 1176, and by the 1300s it supported many shops – which led to the addition of another verse, that we have not included here, 'Build it up with silver and gold'. The bridge survived the Great Fire of London in 1666, but its foundations were weakened. The latest re-build was in the 1960s, the previous one having been transported to Arizona, USA, brick by brick.

The Israelites continued to disobey God, and eventually God allowed Babylon to attack and completely destroy their land, razing the capital city, Zion (Jerusalem) to the ground. Most of its inhabitants were killed, and others were exiled to Babylon. Only a few were left in the devastated city, whose walls were torn down and destroyed by fire.

Nehemiah, a prophet, was sent to Babylon. He was promoted to King's cup bearer and heard of the fate of Jerusalem. The king, noting his sadness, asked him what the matter was. Nehemiah explained, and the king allowed him to go back to Jerusalem and re-build the walls. The king even gave him letters to provide him with safe passage.

Nehemiah met fierce opposition and taunting, especially from Sanballat, but he remained determined to finish his re-building project. He proved to be an inspiring leader always encouraging his men to remember their God. Despite discontent and grumbling from the workers, Nehemiah persevered, exercising justice at all times.

14A

Zion's walls were falling down,
Falling down, falling down.
Hence his sad and worried frown.
Nehemiah.

So the king said, "You go back,
You go back, you go back.
Here are letters for your pack,
Nehemiah!"

Sanballat just laughed and mocked,
Laughed and mocked, laughed and mocked.
"You can't build with crumbled rock!
Nehemiah!"

But he worked, and blessed the Lord,
Blessed the Lord, blessed the Lord;
Holding spear and bow and sword.
Nehemiah!

Working hard, he acted fair,
Acted fair, acted fair;
Made his enemies despair,
Nehemiah!

Eventually the walls were restored and there were huge celebrations. Ezra, the priest, then read to them from the Book of the Law, in which God laid out His instructions as to how they should live. All the people confessed their sins and promised to obey God in the future.

Nehemiah's courage and faith should inspire us to obey God in a world where lack of faith has led to so much destruction.

Nehemiah 1 - 13

Zion's wall were soon rebuilt,
Soon rebuilt, soon rebuilt;
Trusting God he did not wilt.
Nehemiah

Ezra read the Law out loud,
Law out loud, law out loud;
"We'll obey the Lord," they vowed.
"Nehemiah."

And today, faith's falling down,
Falling down, falling down;
So, with hope and prayer abound,
And inspire!

15

Wee Willie Winkie

Runs through the town,

Upstairs, downstairs

In his night gown;

Knocking at the window,

Crying through the lock,

"Are the children all in bed?

It's past eight o'clock!"

We may complain about political interference these days, but it is nothing compared with the new laws introduced in 1841, when this rhyme was written by William Miller. The police force was relatively new and it was decided that, 'for the good of the people', a curfew should be introduced! As you can imagine, this was not popular with liberal minded folk who thought their bed time was no-one else's business! This rhyme may well have been an ironical comment on this new curfew.

As there were no newspapers or radios at that time, the Town Crier would go through the town ringing a bell and shouting his messages, making sure everyone heard and understood.

There are times when we can feel very alone, feeling that no-one hears or cares what we say, or feel and we want to shout out all our feelings.

There are a collection of songs in the Bible called the *Psalms*. Many were written by King David when he was being hunted and attacked. They are the genuine, heart-felt cries of men who sometimes did not understand what God was doing. However, despite their doubts and uncertainties, the one solid confidence they had was that God was in control, loved them, and would eventually protect them. They too needed to rest, but in the promises of God, and not in their beds!

15A

We will be thinking,

Once we are 'down',

"Who shares our cares

That we might drown?"

Knocked by all our sin, though

Crying, we'll take stock;

For the children God has led

Stand fast on His rock!

This *God song,* and the next two, reflects some of the emotions that the psalmists were going through. This particular one echoes David's fear that he would be overcome by his suffering and that God no longer heard him when he cried out for help. He cries to God out of the realisation of the enormity of his sin, and the fear that it would overwhelm him. But his ultimate confidence was that God was his refuge and strength, and He alone was the safe and secure rock on which to shelter.

Psalm 13 v 1 - 2, 5 - 6

Psalm 69 v 15

Psalm 130 v 3

Psalm 61 v 1 - 2

16

Sing a song of sixpence,

A pocket full of rye.

Four and twenty blackbirds

Baked in a pie.

When the pie was opened

The birds began to sing.

Now wasn't that a dainty dish

To set before the king?

There is an Italian recipe book from 1549 which has a recipe 'to make pies so that birds may be alive in them and fly out when it is cut up'. It was sometimes used by cooks in England as a novel and amusing part of a royal banquet.

Just as the singing birds were a dainty dish to set before the king in England, so our singing hearts are a 'dainty dish' to offer to God.

David was a musician, and wrote many psalms praising God, though he was always aware that he really did not have adequate words to express the glory of God. In this next song we too pray for the words and the ability to offer God the worship due to Him, even though we are sinful and inadequate. Our worship always delights Him.

16A

Sing a song to Jesus,
Our Rock, and Lord most high!
Or if any lack words,
Make this your cry;
"May my eyes be opened,
May words of praise I sing!
Because, though not a saint, I wish
To let my Lord be King!"

Psalm 95 v 1

Psalm 96 v 1

Psalm 71 v 15

Psalm 19 v 12 – 14

Psalm 10 v 16

17

Ring a ring o' roses;

A pocket full of posies;

A'tishoo! A'tishoo!

We all fall down!

It is often claimed that these words refer to the bubonic plague of 1340s or the Great plague of London in 1665, the 'rings' referring to the ring-like rash on the skin, the posies to bundles of herbs carried around for protection, and the sneezing to the last symptom of the disease before the afflicted person died. This is disputed, however, as the first written record of the rhyme was in 1881 and far too late to refer back to the plague! It is, nevertheless, an interesting possible origin.

Lots of things can make us 'fall down'. Certainly, as in the story of Job, illness and loss can knock us down very easily. The psalms are full of questions from men who had been knocked down by difficult circumstances, but David found that sometimes the questioning had to stop and his attention had to return to the promises of God. When he began to walk with God again, he found that his questions diminished, and his confidence in God and His love grew. As a result his spirits were lifted.

17A

Bring the King your poses;
You've buckets of 'suppose?'s
"What if you? What if you?"
We all fall down!

Cling to things He shows us;
Our Rock, His love o'erflows us!
He lifts you, He lifts you!
We all get up!

Psalm 77 v 7 - 9, 11, 15

Psalm 25 v 6

Psalm 63 v 8

Psalm 31 v 2 - 5

Psalm 30 v 11

Psalm 33 v 11, 15, 20 – 22

18

There was a crooked man

Who walked a crooked mile;

He found a crooked sixpence

Upon a crooked style.

He had a crooked cat

Who found a crooked mouse;

They all lived together

In a little crooked house.

This refers back to the times of the English Stuart King Charles I, and the 'crooked man' is thought to be Sir Alexander Leslie who managed to get an agreement which secured the political and religious freedom of the Scots. The 'crooked style' is thought to refer to the English/Scottish border, and the reference to them all living together in a little crooked house alludes to the uneasy agreement between them.

We often refer to evil people as 'crooked', and if we are really honest we can see something of this crookedness in all of us. We have seen throughout the Old Testament the story of God's special people constantly rebelling against God and disobeying Him. We have read of the prophets whom God sent to bring them back to Him, and how they failed time and time again. But all through the Old Testament is the promise that things will change, that a 'Messiah', a special messenger from God, would come and rescue the situation, and bring a new message of hope to God's people. This next song is about John the Baptist whom God sent to announce that at last the Messiah had arrived, and He could put right all the wrongs in the world and in people's lives. He alone could straighten all that was crooked in the world.

18A

There was a crooked man
Who had a crooked wife;
Bad thoughts and crooked actions
Led to a crooked life.
They had some crooked kids,
Round whom, what's crooked swirled;
They all lived together
In a sad and crooked world

The true man up in Heav'n
Sent John to pave the way,
To straighten out the highway,
Prepare for true Man's day.
So all the crooked kids,
The man and crooked wife,
Could all live together
In a new and straightened life.

Proverbs 21 v 8

Romans 2 v 21 - 32

Matthew 3 v 1 - 17

Romans 5 v 15 - 19

19

Hark, hark, the dogs do bark;

The beggars are coming to town;

Some in rags, and some in jags,

And one in a velvet gown.

This rhyme paints a picture of its 13th century social situation. The 'beggars' were often wandering minstrels, going from town to town spreading news, or, more sinisterly, subversive calls to revolt. Secret messages of dissent were often camouflaged within their songs, leading to plots and uprising against the rich and powerful members of the community, such as royalty, priests and politicians.

The fact that the dogs barked in warning may reflect the unwelcome nature of these wanderers, who were often vagabonds and trouble-makers. This was especially true in the time of the Great Plague, when strangers were thought to be carriers of the disease.

The beggars in this *odd song* may have been bringing news, but in the *God song* we read of some truly spectacular news - not announced by beggars, but by angels! Their news was that a very special person, the Messiah, had been born. This song celebrates the way the angels in Heaven announced Jesus' birth in Bethlehem to the shepherds in the fields. He invites everyone – rich or poor, to come and worship Him, and to make Him King of their lives.

19A

Hark, hark, how angels mark
That Jesus is coming to town!
"Come you lads, and shepherd dads
Seek One in a swaddling gown."

Hark, hark, how in your heart,
God begs you to come and bow down.
Those in rags, or driving jags,
Just come and King Jesus crown!

Luke 2 v 8 - 11

Galatians 3 v 28 - 29

Philippians 2 v 10

Revelation 11 v 15 – 16

20

Little boy blue, come blow your horn!

The sheep's in the meadow,

The cow's in the corn.

Where is the boy who looks after the sheep?

He's under the haystack fast asleep.

Will you awake him? No, not I!

For if I do, he's sure to cry!

This rhyme was first printed in *Tommy Thumb's Song Book* 1744, but there is a theory that 'Little Boy Blue' could be Cardinal Wolsey (1475 – 1530). Wolsey was a very rich, arrogant, self-made man, who was extremely unpopular. He was known as 'Boy Batchelor' after obtaining a degree from Oxford at 15 years old. The phrase 'come blow your horn' may be referring to his bragging and 'blowing his own trumpet' as we might say. In an ostentatious display of wealth and power he transformed a medieval manor into the magnificent Hampton Court Palace.

The words 'Where's the boy who looks after the sheep?' could refer to him being more concerned about getting rich, than about looking after the country, and the rhyme may have been the people's voice of dissent. The title 'Little Boy Blue' may refer to the blue faces of four leopards on Cardinal Wolsey's coat of Arms.

Here is another *God song* about the birth of Jesus. This one refers back to the promise in the Old Testament that the Messiah would be like a shepherd who comes to seek his lost sheep. Only He would not be the sort of shepherd who drops off to sleep and forgets to look after his sheep! And yet, although He is King of the universe, He was to be found as a baby lying in a manger.

20A

Listen! It's true! Come blow your horn!

The sheep need a shepherd,

And now He's been born.

Where is the one who'll look after His sheep?

He lies in a manger fast asleep.

Will you adore Him? Tell me why?

'Cos He's your King, the Lord most high!

Matthew 9 v 36

Zechariah 10 v 2

John 10 v 11

Luke 2 v 8 - 15, 20

21

Christmas is coming,

The geese are getting fat!

Please put a penny

In the old man's hat.

If you haven't got a penny

A ha'penny will do;

If you haven't got a ha'penny

Then God bless you!

The purpose of this little rhyme is purely moral! It encouraged people to remember the poor at Christmas time, and to give charitably. If they themselves were poor then God's blessing was called down upon them.

In the world of today that concentrates so much on the commercial and material side of Christmas, it is good to be reminded that when Jesus came to earth He gave up everything for our sakes.

21A

Christmas is coming,
The gifts attest to that!
We've got so many
In our Santa's sack.
Jesus hadn't got a penny,
He gave all for you,
So that you can be forgiven
And God bless you!

Philippians 2 v 6 - 8

Matthew 8 v 20

Romans 5 v 16

22

Little Jack Horner

Sat in the corner

Eating his Christmas pie.

He put in his thumb

And pulled out a plum,

And said, 'What a good boy am I!"

This sounds such an innocent rhyme, but its origin probably lies in bribery, deceit, theft and execution!

Jack Horner was thought to live during the reign of King Henry VIII, when monasteries and Abbeys were being ransacked and ruined. Horner was reputed to be steward to Richard Whiting, the Bishop of Glastonbury, who boasted the largest and wealthiest abbey in England. In 1539 it was the only monastery still standing, and Whiting realised time was running out for him, so he tried to bribe King Henry to leave it alone.

He sent Horner to the King with 12 title deeds to various grand English estates. As was often the custom, they were hidden inside a pie in order to thwart potential thieves. One theory is that Horner stole one of the title deeds – that to the Manor of Mells – the 'plum' estate of them all. It may, however, have been given to him as a reward for helping to convict the Bishop when, as a member of the jury, he condemned the Bishop to be hung, drawn and quartered on Glastonbury Tor.

The Manor of Mells became the property of the Horner family, who lived there until the 20th century.

This adaptation of the rhyme reminds us that Jesus did not come into the world just for the good people. He came for so called "good", and bad alike, because He loves us all so much, and we all need forgiving.

22A

Little Jack Horner
Sat in the corner
Eating his Christmas pie.
He thought of the room
He'd swept with a broom,
And said, "What a good boy am I!"

Little Jack Horner
Sat in the corner
Eating his Christmas pie.
He thought of his spite,
His temper and bite,
And said, "What a bad boy am I!"

Little Jack Horner
Sat in the corner,
Eating his Christmas pie.
He thought of God's Son
And how He had come,
And said, "What a loved boy am I!"

Romans 7 v 18 – 25

John 3 v 16

23

Twinkle, twinkle little star;

How I wonder what you are!

Up above the world so high,

Like a diamond in the sky.

Twinkle, twinkle little star;

How I wonder what you are!

This was first published by Jane and Ann Taylor in 1806, in a book called *Rhymes for the Nursery*. It encourages the use of simile and imagination and is often used as a lullaby to help children get off to sleep.

The coming of Jesus was announced by the angels to the poor shepherds, but this next song tells us how the rich and great were also led to find Him. A special, unusually bright star was used to lead wise astrologers from the East, to Bethlehem where the young Jesus was living.

23A

Twinkle, twinkle great big star;

What a wonder! So bizarre!

Up above the world so high,

Hear its message from the sky.

"Twinkle, twinkle!" says the star;

"Here's the One you've sought from far!"

Matthew 2 v 1, 2, 9, 10

24

Cobbler, cobbler, mend my shoe!

Get it done by half past two.

Half past two is much too late!

Get it done by half past eight.

Nothing is known about the history of this rhyme, except that it is American, and thought to be a means of teaching children to tell the time.

Just as the cobbler had to watch the time, so did the wise men, who had to find the exact time and place of the birth of the new King.

When King Herod heard from the wise men that a very special baby, who was to be a king, had been born, he was furious. He was so mad that he ordered all children under two years old to be massacred so that he could be certain that there could be no rival to his throne. God, however, had warned Jesus' parents to escape, and they fled to Egypt taking little Jesus with them, and so escaped the slaughter.

After Herod had died, the family returned to Nazareth where Jesus grew up in obedience to both God and his parents. Though He never became the sort of king that Herod had imagined, He certainly is King of the universe, and deserves our total submission as King in our lives.

24A

Toddler, toddler, under two,
Scriptures long foretold of you.
Wise men searched to know the date;
Used a star to navigate.

Toddler, toddler under two,
Herod heard from them of you.
Jealous of his kingly state,
Rivals he'd not tolerate.

Toddler, toddler, under two;
In a rage King Herod flew.
Time and place he'd correlate;
Plan how he could seal your fate.

Toddlers, toddlers all of you,
Every one, King Herod slew,
Screamed in fury, rage and hate,
"Rival king? - Exterminate!"

Toddler, toddler under two,

God's own Son, God rescued you.

Sent to Egypt, there to wait;

Herod's death to celebrate.

Toddler, toddler, as you grew,

Perfect grace in God you knew.

God in man you demonstrate,

His great love, communicate.

Now we come to worship you

Who in God in stature grew,

Now as King we re-instate;

All we are to you donate.

Matthew 2

Luke 2 v 40

25

Hey diddle, diddle,

The cat and the fiddle,

The cow jumped over the moon!

The little dog laughed

To see such sport

And the dish ran away with the spoon!

One possible and plausible origin for this rhyme dates back to 1765, and describes an old-fashioned pub crawl along the A537, Macclesfield to Buxton Road in Derbyshire.

'The cat and the fiddle' may refer to *The Cat and Fiddle Inn*, which is still trading, 'The cow jumped over the moon' to the *Half Moon* pub, which ceased trading long ago, and 'The little dog laughed to see such fun' to *The Setter Dog* public house, built in 1740, which ceased trading in 2002. 'And the dish ran away with the spoon' may well be a reference to *The Dish and Spoon* public house, which in very recent years changed its name to *Peak View Tearooms*. The pubs are about 6 miles apart. Perhaps the imbibing of all that ale resulted in the merriment and jumping over the moon!

The *Hey Diddle Diddle* rhyme may have been nonsense - but it must have seemed equally nonsensical to the leaders of the Jewish religion for Jesus to claim to be the Messiah.

When Jesus was a young man he used to go into the temple and read the Scriptures (now known as our Old Testament). One day He read out loud a passage from the prophet Isaiah that looked forward to the coming of the Messiah. It told how He would heal the sick, and set the captives free. Jesus declared that these words were being fulfilled before their very eyes. His hearers had seen the amazing healings that He had performed, and Jesus was now telling them that this was confirmation that He was indeed the promised Messiah.

Hey diddle, diddle,

How's that for a riddle?

The 'cowed' are over the moon!

The under-dog laughs,

For Jesus taught

That this mish-mash of 'failures' would bloom!

Hey diddle, diddle!

We're back to this riddle!

For now deaf come and hear more!

The cripples run fast!

Blind see! Dumb talk!

And He dished out good news to the poor!

Hey diddle, diddle

To facts in this riddle

They found the prophets were tuned.

Though this was long past,

Now Jesus brought

All they'd wished for, and prayed would come soon.

Matthew 11 v 4 - 5

Luke 4 v 14 - 21

26

See-saw, Margery Daw,

Johnny shall have a new master.

He shall have but a penny a day,

Because he can't work any faster.

There is no evidence that there was an actual historical person called Margery Daw, though Marjory was a name almost exclusively used by poor country people in the 18th and 19th centuries and 'Daw' is defined in the Oxford English dictionary as 'a lazy person, sluggard'. It was co-incidentally useful in that it rhymed with 'saw'!

The rhyme reflects the use of child labour in work houses where those with nowhere else to live would be forced to work for a pittance (a penny a day) on piece work (because he can't work any faster). The words of *See-saw Margery Daw* might have been used by a spiteful child to taunt another, implying his family was destined for the workhouse.

The rhyme may have origins as a work song for sawyers, helping them to keep the rhythm when using a two-person saw.

In the 18th and 19th centuries a servant's whole existence depended on who happened to be his master. Jesus knew how crucial it was to serve the right person, and He explained that one can only serve one master - be it God or money. The choice is ours!

26A

See-saw, Margery Daw,

Some day she'll have a new master.

She may serve all her pennies each day,

And then as she works they'll grow faster.

See saw, Margery Daw,

Will she choose God as her Master?

She's aware that there's many a day,

His love helps her cope with disaster.

See saw, Margery Daw

Cannot serve both as her master.

One she'd hate and the other obey;

And always do all that he asked her.

Matthew 6:24

27

It's raining, it's pouring,

The old man is snoring.

He bumped his head

On the end of the bed

And couldn't get up in the morning!

Little is known for certain about the origin of this rhyme – though one would think it's bound to have been in 'weather preoccupied' England! It is a chant often sung by children when they are unable to go out to play because of the rain.

This song is not found before the mid-twentieth century in the USA. It was noted in 1939 in New York by Charles Ives (1874–1954) and copyrighted in 1944 by Freda Selicoff.

One possible suggestion is that it was written about the meteorologist John Dalton. On July 27th 1844, after suffering several previous strokes, he made his last meteorological observation (presumably that it was raining!)

Jesus taught that prayer is vital if we are to follow Him closely, but it takes determination and discipline, especially when we feel it would be so much easier to stay in bed!

27A

It's raining, it's pouring,

The old man is snoring.

Get out of bed

And get praying instead;

You shouldn't let up in the morning!

Matthew 26 v 41

28

Three blind mice! Three blind mice!

See how they run! See how they run!

They all run after the farmer's wife,

Who cut off their tails with a carving knife.

Did ever you see such a sight in your life

As three blind mice?

Queen Mary I, known as 'Bloody Mary', and daughter of King Henry VIII, often features in nursery rhymes, and it would appear that she is commemorated in this one too. She and her husband, King Philip of Spain, owned huge estates, hence why she is referred to as 'the farmer's wife'. She was a Catholic who sought out and persecuted Protestants – often killing them. The 'three blind mice' were protestant bishops, Ridley, Latimer and Cranmer, (known as The Oxford Martyrs), who were convicted of plotting against the Queen, and were subsequently burnt at the stake.

Jesus talked a lot about blindness. He gave sight to many physically blind people, but He also claimed to be able to restore sight to those who were spiritually blind. Jesus claimed to be 'The Light of the World'. He knew that men (and women!) live in darkness – not knowing what is right and what is wrong, what is best for them, or what is harmful. Much that attracts us leads us into pain and trouble.

God created light, He is the source of light, and through Jesus offers to dispel that darkness that haunts us, and lead us to truth and real joy.

28A

Three blind guys! Three blind guys,
See how they run! See how they run!
They all run after a 'charmer's' life;
With all that entails, causing harm and strife.
They never could see it unhinges their life;
These three blind guys.

Re-mind guys, re-mind guys
Where they should run; where they should run.
Should all run after the Father's light;
He plucks off their scales and imparts new sight.
For ever they'll see that this brings great delight!
Let's re-mind guys!

Romans 1 v 18 - 32

2 Corinthians 4 v 3 - 6

Genesis 1 v 3

John 8 v 12

29

Little Tommy Tucker

Sings for his supper.

What will you give him?

Brown bread and butter.

This rhyme was first published in 1829, and refers to the many orphans (often collectively known as 'Tommy Tuckers') who had to beg for their food by singing. The second half of the rhyme, which is not included in this book, says, 'How shall he cut it without a knife? How shall he marry without a wife?' This draws attention to his poverty, and the unlikelihood of him ever being able to find a wife and get married.

One of the things Jesus emphasised to His followers was how much His Father God loved them and wanted to care for them. He pointed out that if they, as mere human fathers, knew how to feed their children properly, care for them, and treat them well, how much more their Father in Heaven would shower all sorts of wonderful gifts onto His children. He promised they would never lack anything that was good for them.

29A

Little Tommy Tucker
Sings for his supper.
What will you give him?
Brown bread and butter.

Never would you offer
Stones for his supper,
Rather than give him
Cakes and a cuppa!

Yet your love is but a
Shade of God's utter
Love for His children.
Wow! What a papa!

Matthew 7 v 9 - 11

30

Hark, hark, the dogs do bark,

The beggars are coming to town;

Some in rags, and some in jags,

And one in a velvet gown.

For the history of this rhyme see number 19.

We may distinguish between social classes, from beggars to those in velvet gowns, but God doesn't! He makes no distinction. Jesus was anxious to convey how much God loves and cares for all His creatures. He showers His love and protection on birds and flowers, which are so transient, so how much more will He protect and care for us, His children? Jesus told us that He knows all His creation intimately - from whether a sparrow falls, to how many hairs we have on our heads, and He feeds and cares for us all.

30A

Hark, hark! How God loves larks,
And sparrows that come into town.
Clothes and feeds and meets their needs;
Each one He has noted down.

Hark, hark, when Christ remarks
On lilies that grow on the ground;
None can sow, or plough or hoe;
Such beauty is rarely found!

Hark, hark, how Christ embarks
On sharing God's care so profound;
I'm preferred to flocks of birds;
He numbers the hairs on my crown.

Matthew 6 v 25 - 33

Luke 12 v 6 - 7

31

One man went to mow,

Went to mow a meadow.

One man and his dog, Spot, bottle of pop,

Old mother Reilly and her cow,

They went to mow a meadow.

This is a popular song, which, because each verse increases the number of men who go to mow, is used to teach children how to count.

Just as in this rhyme, one man is joined by another, and then another and so on, so Jesus, just before He went back up to Heaven, commissioned His followers to make more disciples. He told them to spread the good news of His love and forgiveness to everyone in the world – and they obeyed. For some it meant persecution and death, but if they had not gone out and sowed the seed of the Gospel, we may never have heard. Now it's our responsibility to continue to spread this life-saving message to all who will listen.

31A

One man went to sow,

Went to sow the gospel.

One man and his God, - not - "What've I got?

Oh bother, really, not me now!"

But, "Yes! I'll sow the Gospel!"

That's how I can know,

I can know the Gospel.

One man, and his God, spots, "That'll be what

All others really need right now,"

And so they shared the Gospel.

So now let us go;

Let us share the Gospel.

Let us trust our God, not bottle the lot,

"Nobody really needs to know,"

But, "Let us share the Gospel!"

Matthew 28 v 18 - 20

32

Hickory Dickory Dock!

The mouse ran up the clock.

The clock struck one

The mouse ran down.

Hickory Dickory Dock!

This was a favourite rhyme of Sir Walter Scott who used to recite it to Marjorie Fleming, the diarist. It is thought to be useful for introducing children to the concept of telling the time.

The 'tick-tock' of the clock reminds us that time is passing. Jesus knew that time was short for Him to teach people, so He made sure He did it in the most effective way! He not only taught in plain and simple words, but He often taught in pictures, called parables. This helped to illustrate some of his wonderful truths in terms that the local listeners could understand. His disciples also used picture language in their later letters.

This rhyme includes two of the pictures used by Jesus, and two later ones used by His followers. Jesus drew the parallel between the lives of the people around Him, and the building of a house, questioning whether the house of their lives was built on a firm foundation or not. Another time he talked of the separation of people as a shepherd would separate sheep from goats, the former being chosen to live, and the latter being rejected. We read of life described as a race, when the participants need to press forward with determination. Finally, a picture is drawn of Jesus as a visitor outside a locked door – knocking patiently to see if He is admitted or not. These are some of the vignettes used in the Bible to help us understand some of God's truths.

Hebrews 12 v 1

Matthew 7 v 24 - 27

Matthew 25 v 32 - 46

Revelation 3 v 20

32A

Hickory Dickory Dock!
Your life runs like a clock.
When time is done,
And race is run,
Will you be quickest, or not?

Hickory Dickory Dock!
The storm comes as a shock!
When rains beats down,
And you could drown.
Built on the silt or the rock?

Hickory Dickory Dock!
The shepherd sorts his flock.
"Sheep! In you come!
You goats go down!"
Which of the pick is your lot?

This is a visitor's knock
You daren't ignore or mock.
Christ stands before
Your heart's closed door.
Click the key quick, and unlock.

33

Three little kittens,
They lost their mittens,
So they began to cry,
"Oh, Mother dear,
Come here, come here,
For we have lost our mittens."
"Lost your mittens!
You naughty kittens!
Then you shall have no pie."
"Mee-ow, mee-ow, we shall have no pie!"

Three little kittens
They found their mittens,
So they began to cry,
"Oh, Mother dear,
Come here, come here,
For we have found our mittens!"
"Found your mittens!
You good little kittens!
Then you shall have some pie!"
"Prrrr! Prrrr! We shall have some pie!"

33A

One loving daddy,

He lost his laddie

When he said his goodbye.

He swapped career

For girls and beer

And quite forgot his daddy.

This young laddie

Forgot his daddy

For he lived life so high;

See how, see how, he lived life so high.

This young sonny

He lost his money,

And thought that he would die.

"Oh! Deary dear,

I'll starve, I fear!

For I have lost my money!

Life's not funny,

Yet Dad's got money,

To work for him, I'll try.

See now! See now! To work for him I'll try."

This is probably just a reminder to children to look after things! The first known publication of the song is in Eliza Follen's book *New Nursery songs for All Good Children* (1787 - 1860), but she describes it here as a 'traditional' song, implying that it dates back much further.

Jesus often talked of people being lost, and of God trying to find them. One picture He used to illustrate this was that of a lost son. This son wanted his inheritance early, and his father gave it to him. He then went to a far away country where he spent all his money on riotous living. When he had spent his fortune, and was destitute, he decided to go back to his father and ask for his forgiveness and offer to work for him for a living. This song describes the incredible love of the father, as he welcomes his returning son with open arms.

Jesus was likening His listeners to the lost son, and the father to God - demonstrating the enormous love of God who longs to welcome back and forgive anyone who returns to Him in repentance.

33A *continued*

But when this laddie

Came back to daddy

Dad ran to him and cried,

"Oh son, most dear,

Come here, come here,

For I have missed my laddie."

So this daddy

Just hugged his laddie,

To him no treat denied.

"See now! See now! He's alive, who died."

Luke 15 v 11 – 32

34A

Old King Cole

Was a merry old soul,

And a merry old soul was he!

He called for his pipe,

And he called for his bowl,

And he called for his fiddlers three.

Some think that the origin of this rhyme was based on a Celtic King called Cole who lived in 3rd century AD. Legend has it that when he was Duke of Caercolun he organized a rebellion against King Asclepiod, whom he killed in battle. He then assumed the monarchy himself, and re-named Caercolun, Colechester, meaning Cole's Camp. We now know it as Colchester. (In Latin, the word for camp is 'castrum' which later became 'chester' in English.)

Cole came to an agreement with the Romans that he would be subject to them and pay taxes in exchange for being able to retain the Kingdom of Britain. One month later he died, and Constantius, a Roman senator, married his daughter Helen, and replaced Cole as King of Britain. They had a son whom they called Constantine, who later became the Emperor known as Constantine the Great.

Christ's message has nothing to do with seeking power, nor is it anything to do with miserable religion! Jesus talked about celebrations and parties. He told the story of a King who sent out invitations to his friends, but they were too busy or too pre-occupied to come. So he extended the invitation to all and sundry - beggars and homeless, out in the highways and byways. Jesus likened this to God's invitation to us to be part of His Kingdom festivities. No one is too poor or too bad to get an invitation to God's wonderful ball.

34A

Old King Cole

Was a merry old soul,

And yet merrier souls are we!

God calls - not His 'type',

But he calls to us all;

At His ball He is bidding us be!

Matthew 22 v 1 - 10

35

Doctor Foster went to Gloucester

In a shower of rain.

He stepped in a puddle

Right up to his middle,

And never went there again.

Although the first published version of this rhyme was in the 19th century, it is thought that the word 'puddle' in the rhyme may have originally been 'piddle', meaning 'stream', as this rhymes more accurately with middle. If this is the case then the rhyme must have had its origins much further back.

It is suggested that King Edward I, King of England in the 13th century, was known as Doctor Foster. It is reputed that he went to Gloucester, which is on the banks of the River Severn, and is liable to flooding. He apparently fell off his horse into a puddle (or stream?) and was so angry that he vowed he would never return.

The rhyme was also used to warn children against playing in puddles, which could be very deep in the unmade roads of yesteryear!

Doctor Foster may have been put off by mishaps, but God certainly isn't! He never gives up!

Here is another *God song* about something that was lost – a gold coin from a very precious wedding dowry that would have been worn around a lady's forehead. Jesus describes how the distraught owner would clean the room and search high and low until she found the coin. He likens that search to the lengths to which God goes to find those of us who are lost to Him, and talks of the celebrations in Heaven when a lost sinner is found.

35A

Lady lost a coin that cost her
Many hours of pain.
She swept up her muddle;
Quite sure that she did all,
(What*ever*!) to wear 't again!

God still searches, and His church is
Full of 'lost - re-claimed'.
With rapture He'll bid all,
"Play trumpet and fiddle!
They'll never despair again!"

Luke 15 v 8 - 10

36

Jack be nimble, Jack be quick!

Jack jump over the candlestick!

This ditty was first known to be published in 1798. It is thought to be connected to the old tradition of leaping first over fires, and then, with safety in mind, over candles!

It was both a sport and a method of fortune telling, and it was thought that a year's good luck would follow a successful leap without extinguishing the candle.

It was particularly popular in Wendover where there were lace-making schools. Here it was traditional to dance around the lace-makers' great candlestick and this led to jumping over it. Due to the cost of candles some employers only allowed the use of candles during the darkest months of the year, known as the candle season, which centred around Candlemas Day.

Jesus also talked about candles and candlesticks. He reminded folk that there is no point putting a candle in a basket and shutting the lid! It needs to be set on a candlestick and put somewhere where people can see the light. That's how it should be for His followers – they are to be shining lights to all those around them, so that their good deeds can be seen, and God be praised.

36A

Jack was simple, Jack was thick,
Jack, he covered his candle wick.

Jack, be nimble, Jack be quick!
Jack it up on a candlestick!

Jack be gentle, Jack be good!
Jack! Shine out as your candle should!

Jack! Let those who lack your ways
Jack sin in, and then give God praise.

Matthew 5 v 15 - 16

37

Mary, Mary, quite contrary,

How does your garden grow?

With silver bells and cockle shells

And pretty maids all in a row.

The true origin of this rhyme, and the meaning of the different elements, is uncertain. Mary could be Mary Queen of England or of Scotland; the 'bells' could refer to the bells of Catholic cathedrals; 'Cockle shells' may allude to the infidelity of Mary, Queen of Scots' husband, and the 'Pretty maids all in a row', to her ladies in waiting. 'How does your garden grow?' may be making reference to Mary I's barren womb, and 'quite contrary' to her determination to reverse the ecclesiastical changes made by her father, King Henry VIII.

However, the most gruesome, likely suggestion is that this is the Catholic Queen Mary Tudor, ('Bloody Mary'), who martyred many Protestants. The 'garden' then refers to the graveyards which grew in number to accommodate all her martyrs. 'Silver bells' and 'cockle shells' were colloquialisms for instruments of torture – thumb screws, and similar instruments attached to the genitals! The 'maids' were guillotines (originally known as 'maidens'), used to decapitate Mary's victims.

Jesus often used the picture of sowing, planting, and reaping to illustrate the way His message is planted in our hearts. He told the story of a farmer sowing seed that fell in a variety of places and likened it to the seed of the good news of God which, when spread around, will be heard by all sorts of people. Some people's hearts will be shallow and unreceptive (like paths, where the seeds are eaten by birds). Others will not stay the course when things get tough (like shallow soil, where the seeds are scorched by the sun). Some will be too caught up with riches and pleasure for God's message to survive (choked by weeds), but at other times the good news will be received with such joy that it flourishes, grows and multiplies. This next song describes the different soils about which Jesus talks.

37A

Mary, Mary, quite contrary,
How does your garden grow?
The seed that fell on paths as well
Were eaten by sparrow and crow.

Mary, Mary, quite contrary,
How does your garden grow?
In shallow soil, despite your toil,
The seeds would be scorched, as you know.

Mary, Mary, quite contrary,
How does your garden grow?
For if the seeds fell in the weeds,
Their roots would be choked from below.

Mary, Mary, not contrary,
How does your garden grow?
Your seeds took birth in fertile earth,
Producing a wonderful show!

Matthew 13 v 3 - 8
Matthew 13 v 38 - 39

38

Baa Baa black sheep,

Have you any wool?

Yes sir, yes sir,

Three bags full!

One for the master

And one for the dame,

And one for the little boy

Who lives down the lane.

This rhyme may have been used to teach children where wool comes from, and also the sounds made by sheep.

Historically, though, it is thought to be associated with the tax imposed on the wool industry in the 13th century. The 'Master' would have been King Edward, to whom went one third of the profits. A second third went to the church (the Dame), and the last third went to the farmer (the little boy).

In our *God songs*, this is the first of a trilogy of shepherd songs where Jesus likens Himself to a shepherd, and His listeners to sheep. Here we sing of the sheep who had broken God's rules and wandered away, and learn how the shepherd searched for him until he was found, and then carried him home with great joy. We are told in Isaiah that God knows us by name.

38A

Baa Baa black sheep,

Have you been a fool?

Yes sir, yes sir,

Broke God's rule.

Come, here's the Shepherd

Who calls you by name;

And home, in His arms with joy,

He'll bring you again!

Luke 15 v 4 - 7

Isaiah 43 v 1

117

39

Mary had a little lamb,

Its fleece was white as snow;

And everywhere that Mary went

The lamb was sure to go.

It followed her to school one day;

That was against the rule.

It made the children laugh and play

To see a lamb at school

This is an American song, written by Sarah Hale, of Boston, in 1830, which has somehow found its way into our English tradition. It is used educationally to introduce children to similes (white as snow). No specific historical connection can be traced, but it is interesting that the words of this rhyme were the first words ever recorded by Thomas Edison on his phonograph.

Most lambs don't follow so devotedly! It is more natural for them to wander away – and so it is with Jesus' 'lambs', who prefer to go their own way to following the Shepherd. But this song tells of how much Jesus loves the wandering lamb and wants to forgive him and bring him back to a close walk with Him. Isaiah tells us that our sins will be washed as white as snow, and Jesus tells us that His 'lambs' will then follow more closely because they recognise their Master's voice.

39A

Jesus had a little lamb,

Its heart was black as soot;

And everywhere this bad lamb went

A wrong foot it would put.

It followed its own willful way;

Time and again, a fool!

It made some others go astray,

And couldn't stand God's rule.

Jesus loved this little lamb,

And washed it white as snow;

Then everywhere that Jesus went

The lamb was sure to go.

It followed Him so close each day,

And tried hard not to fall.

And, 'cos it didn't want to stray,

It listened for His call.

Romans 1 v 21 - 32

Roman 4 v 7 - 8

Isaiah 1 v 18

John 14 v 3 - 4

40

Little Bo Peep

Has lost her sheep

And doesn't know

Where to find them.

Leave them alone

And they'll come home

Dragging their tails behind them.

Bo peep is referred to in Shakespeare's *King Lear*, though the rhyme was not published until the 1800s.

It is thought to refer to smuggling, which was rife in the 13th century in St. Leonards, near Hastings. If a smuggler was caught, he was liable to be incarcerated in the Martello Tower (nicknamed 'Little Bo Peep'). This was the official residence of the queen's customs officials. The 'lost sheep' were the smugglers.

Another verse of the rhyme talks of the lambs having left their tails behind them - referring to the smugglers having to abandon their bounty if they thought the customs officials were on to them – and the last verse speaks of little Bo-Peep tacking their tails back on again. This tells of the customs officials trying to link the smugglers up with the goods they had left behind, so that they could successfully apprehend them.

This rhyme is often associated with the baby's game of 'peek-a-boo', (covering one's face and then revealing it quickly).

This third shepherd *God song* tells again of how Jesus came down from Heaven to find His lost sheep and bring them back home, with all their failures forgiven.

40A

Jesus did weep

He lost his sheep

And came down from

Heav'n to find them.

They're not alone

Since they've come home,

Leaving their failures behind them.

Matthew 18 v 12 - 14

Matthew 28 v 20

Romans 6 v 11

41

Ding dong bell,

Pussy's in the well.

Who put her in?

Little Johnny Green.

Who pulled her out?

Little Tommy Stout.

What a naughty boy was that

To try to drown poor pussy cat,

Who never did him any harm,

And killed the mice in his father's barn.

This is an education in moral behaviour. It teaches children that it is unacceptable to be cruel to animals. In the original rhyme the cat was left to drown, but just as we see so much 'political correctness' nowadays, so in 1765, in *Mother Goose's Melody*, this rhyme was altered to the cat being rescued by Tommy Stout!

'Pussy' often referred to a loose woman, as cats were associated with lust, disorderliness and femininity. One possible historical link is the medieval English practice of 'ducking', when the offending woman was paraded through the street. The ringing bells may refer to the noises (including banging pots and pans, and ringing church bells) made during shaming rituals. This would attract the community's attention as the procession made its way to the village pond (well-pond), a focal point of the community. The woman would then be repeatedly lowered into the water by the young men (Johnny Green and Tommy Stout) to show the community's disapproval of her behaviour.

41A

Ding dong bell,

Woman at the well.

Where had she been?

Living in great sin.

Who sought her out?

Jesus - knew about

All her wicked life and that

She tried to drown her guilt with 'chat',

For ever 'hidden', played a 'part',

Not thinking twice that He knew her heart.

Ding dong bell,

Jesus at the well.

What did he say?

Let me drink, I pray!

What did he do?

Said, "I offer you

Living water, which you lack;

And life eternal! For in fact

You'll never heal from all your past

Until you taste of my drink that lasts.

John 14 v 4 - 30

How different was Jesus' attitude when He met the Samaritan woman at the well! She too had lived an immoral life, and because she was ostracised by the general public, she came to the well in the heat of the day, all alone. But Jesus was not a condemning, religious fanatic like those medieval hardliners!

He met her by the well and asked her for some water. The Samaritans were hated by the Jews, and no self-respecting Jew would have been seen in the presence of a Samaritan woman, let alone talk to her and ask her for a favour - and certainly not from a woman of such questionable repute. But Jesus could see her inner pain and thirst, and He wanted to offer her the life-giving water that only He could give. At first she tried to distract Him, with religious talk and 'chat', but He persisted in showing her that He knew all about her, and demonstrated to her that His gift of life was for everyone – including the sinful, ashamed, rejected, and ostracised.

42

There was an old woman

Who lived in a shoe.

She had so many children

She didn't know what to do.

She gave them some broth

Without any bread;

She whipped them all soundly

And sent them to bed.

The 'Old Woman' might have referred to Queen Caroline, wife of King George II, who had eight children or it may refer to King George himself who began the men's fashion for wearing white powdered wigs, and was consequently referred to as the 'old woman'! In this case the children may have been the members of parliament and the bed the Houses of Parliament. The term 'whip' is used today to describe a Member of Parliament whose responsibility it is to ensure that all members 'toe the party line'.

There was an ancient custom of throwing a shoe after the bride as she left for her honeymoon, signifying a wish that she be very fertile. This may link up with the reference to the old woman living in a shoe.

Whatever the historical significance of the old woman one thing was certain, she was distraught, and at a loss to know what to do for the best.

Jesus met someone else who didn't know what to do. He was a rich and good living young ruler. He assured Jesus that he had kept all the rules and regulations that were laid down in the Scriptures, but he was still not sure that he had eternal life. Jesus challenged him to give all his wealth to the poor, and to follow Him in order to find peace with God. This was too hard for the young man, who sadly went away.

42A

There was a rich ruler,
Who lived a good Jew.
He'd kept so many rules, but
He didn't know what to do
To have God's new life.
To which Jesus said,
"Distribute your bounty!
Come follow instead!"

But this wealthy ruler
Had lived to accrue.
He had kept the commandments
But didn't know what to do
To stave off God's wrath.
But when Jesus said,
"Be stripped of your bounty,"
With sadness, he fled.

Matthew 19 v 16 – 22

43

Miss Polly had a dolly who was sick, sick, sick;

She called for the doctor to come quick, quick, quick;

The doctor came with his coat and his hat,

And he knocked on the door with a rat-a-tat tat.

He looked at the dolly and he shook his head;

He said to Miss Polly, "Put her straight to bed!"

He wrote on some paper for a pill, pill, pill,

"I'll be back in the morning with my bill, bill, bill."

Apart from the fact that it clearly dates from before the days of the NHS there is no clear historical link for this rhyme.

We read in the Bible of a rich young man called Jairus, whose daughter was very sick – in fact she died even as her father was pleading with Jesus to go to his home and cure her. Jairus's messengers came to tell Him it was too late, and He might as well go back home. But, to Jesus, death is just like sleeping, and, he told everyone, much to the crowd's scorn, that the little girl was asleep. He then went to her bedside, took her by the hand, and raised her to life again. He told her family to feed her and He gave strict instructions that they should tell no-one what had happened.

Miss Jairus had a virus and was sick, sick, sick.

Dad called out to Jesus to come quick, quick, quick!

But runners came with a note to update,

They were shocked to report "It's too late, oh late, late!"

He took the papyrus, Jesus shook his head.

He said, "No, Miss Jairus is not really dead!

Just note, you'll see later, she's not ill, ill, ill,

You can pack in your mourning; she's asleep still, still!"

"Miss Jairus, please arise as you're no longer sick."

He called back her life, and made her heart to tick.

To people's shame, when He spoke up she sat!

For they'd mocked Him and scorned, "What's He at, oh at, at?"

They looked at Miss Jairus as she raised her head;

She sat, didn't tire as she got out of bed!

Her folk were agape, and marveled till, till, till,

Jesus tacked on this warning "Don't this spill, spill, spill!"

Mark 5 v 22 - 24, 35 - 43

44

Peter, Peter

Pumpkin eater,

Had a wife

And couldn't

Keep her;

Put her in a

Pumpkin shell

And there he kept her

Very well.

In common with some other nursery rhymes, this one originates from the USA. The most popular explanation of this rhyme is that Peter was a poor man whose wife was constantly unfaithful to him. The only way to stop her infidelities was to put her in a chastity belt, signified by the 'pumpkin shell'. In this way he could keep her for himself!

The Peter of the traditional rhyme clearly had trouble controlling his unfaithful wife, and was totally unable to trust her. Peter in the Bible had to learn about trust too, but his difficulty was his own lack of faith. He found it hard to fully believe in Jesus, who was in fact totally trustworthy.

One day, when Peter was out fishing with his friends, he saw Jesus walking on the water, coming towards them. Being impetuous, he believed he could do the same, and jumped out of the boat. Indeed, Jesus had invited him to come, and he could have imitated his Master if he had not suddenly looked at the waves and been filled with fear and doubt. He immediately began to sink. Jesus stretched out and took his hand and saved him. This reminds us of the power of God that is available to us if we would only trust Him completely.

Matthew 14 v 24 - 31

44A

Peter, Peter,
Challenge greeter,
Risked his life
And went to
Meet a
Friend who walked
On water's swell;
He thought that he could
Walk as well.

Peter, Peter,
You have taught us
Look at Christ
And not the
Waters.
When you ceased on
Him to dwell
The tempest raged and
In you fell.

Peter, Peter,
Christ defeats the
Storms of life
And even
Beat the
Power of death
And sin and hell,
And holds your hand, your
Fears to quell.

45

Row, row, row your boat,

Gently down the stream.

Merrily, merrily, merrily, merrily,

Life is just a dream.

Although there were other versions available, the modern version of this song and tune was first recorded in 1881.

It encourages movement and singing in rounds, but there have also been many attempts to impose a moral message on to the words. The boat could be seen as a group working together on 'life's sea' and needing to pull together in a skillful and co-operative way in order to progress.

Jesus lived near Lake Galilee, and many of His followers were fishermen. Sailing and rowing was not always a dream for them, however, as dreadful storms could blow up on the lake very suddenly.

One day the disciples were caught in one such storm, which was so severe that they were in danger of the boat being wrecked. Unlike the terrified sailors, Jesus was sleeping peacefully in the bow! When they woke Him, He once again demonstrated His supreme power over the elements. He simply spoke to the waves and the wind and, to the disciples' utter amazement, the storm stopped.

Luke 8 v 22 - 25

45A

Row, row, row your boat,
Gently with the stream.
Galilee, Galilee, Galilee, Galilee!
Such a peaceful scene!

Oh! No! Boat got soaked,
Rain began to team
Heavily, heavily, heavily, heavily;
It began to lean.

Blow! Blow! Blow! Winds broke
Both the mast and beam.
Scarily, scarily, scarily, scarily!
Certain death was seen.

So, so, so you woke
Jesus, from His dream!
"What if we, what if we, what if we, what if we
Drown here at the scene?"

Lo, lo, lo He spoke
With such power supreme.
Suddenly, suddenly, suddenly, suddenly
All became serene.

"Who, who who's this bloke
Calms the raging sea?
Verily, verily, verily, verily,
God Himself must be!"

46

Oh! Pussy cat, pussy cat,

Where have you been?

I've been to London to visit the queen.

Oh! Pussy cat, pussy cat,

What did you there?

I chased a little mouse under the chair.

This rhyme dates back to 16th century when one of the ladies-in-waiting of Queen Elizabeth I possessed a cat who roamed around Windsor Castle. On one occasion it ran under the Queen's chair. She was startled by it brushing against her leg, but decreed that it should be allowed to roam freely within the castle so long as it rid the building of mice!

When Queen Elizabeth sat on her throne, even her courtiers would have been hesitant to approach her (unlike the said 'pussy cat'!). However this *God song* tells of someone who had no fear of sitting at the feet of Jesus, the King of Kings. What was His reaction to what, in those days, would have appeared to be a scandalous intrusion?

The setting was in the house of two sisters, Martha and Mary. Martha always liked to be busy, cooking and cleaning, whilst Mary preferred to sit at Jesus' feet and learn from Him. Martha complained about Mary, probably both because she was leaving all the work to her, but also because it was unheard of for a woman to invade the privacy of a man, let alone sit beside him and learn from him. Jesus, however, gently rebuked Martha, claiming that Mary had made the right choice, and indicating that all social barriers were broken down in His Kingdom.

46A

So busy that, busy that
Martha could scream!
She's been a-cooking delicious cuisine!
So busy that, busy that,
(Pots everywhere!)
She faced her 'Guest in House', "Do you not care?

So Lazy that, lazy that
Mary has been,
She's been a-chatting while I cook and clean!
So lazy that, lazy that,
Gosh! It's unfair!
I chase around the house; she's by your chair!"

"Oh would you that, would you that
More like her been,
Come here to listen, become more serene.
Oh would you that, would you that,
Whilst I was there,
In place of keeping house, understood prayer"

.

Luke 11 v 38 - 42

47

Ride a cock-horse to Banbury cross,

To see a fine lady upon a white horse;

With rings on her fingers and bells on her toes,

She shall have music wherever she goes.

Some people attribute this rhyme to Queen Elizabeth I who traveled to Banbury to see its huge stone cross. The 'rings on her fingers' were her fine jewelry and the 'bells on her toes' reminds us of the current fashion of the time of having bells on the tips of one's shoes. Since Banbury was at the top of a steep hill the town council made a white stallion available to help pull up the carriage. It is reputed that when the Queen was ascending the hill, a wheel broke on the carriage, and the Queen mounted the horse instead. Minstrels accompanied the procession, giving her 'music wherever she goes.'

Alternatively, the 'fine lady' could refer to Lady Godiva whose husband, Leofric, Earl of Mercia, imposed a heavy tax on his subjects. Godiva, upset by his cruelty, pleaded with him to withdraw the tax. In response, her husband offered a dare that she should ride naked through Coventry, promising he would repeal the law if she did. To his amazement his wife agreed, and galloped through the town on a beautiful white horse. Apparently the townsfolk stayed in their houses behind the shutters to save her blushes! The tax was lifted and Lady Godiva had music (praises of her people) wherever she went!

Jesus didn't choose some stunning white stallion for his entry into Jerusalem. He chose a humble, borrowed colt on which to ride. A week before He was condemned and crucified the crowds hailed Him as their King! But Jesus didn't behave like a human King, in triumph and power. He knew that the crowd would soon change its tone, and yell for his blood, so He set His face resolutely to Jerusalem, determined to suffer death in order to rescue us from Satan's power and the consequences of Hell.

47A

Ride a colt horse to Calvary's Cross,

Oh see our fine Saviour upon a meek horse;

They fling down palm fringes, as well as their clothes;

He shall have music wherever He goes!

Ride a colt horse to Calvary's cross,

But see the crowd change as it gathers in force!

It sings to begin with, then yells with His foes,

"Crucify Jesus!" The clamoring grows.

Ride a colt horse to Calvary's cross;

We see our fine Saviour, full set on His course.

He willingly brings us from hell and its woes;

Hear Heaven's music! In victory He rose!

Luke 19 v 28 - 40

John 12 v 12 - 16

Luke 23 v 18 - 24

Revelations 5 v 11 - 14

48

Pat-a-cake, pat-a-cake,

Baker's man,

Bake me a cake

As fast as you can.

Pat it and prick it

And mark it with 'B',

And put it in the oven

For baby and me.

This rhyme is one of the oldest and most widely known surviving English rhymes. The earliest recorded version appears in Thomas D'Urfey's play *The Campaigners* in 1698.

Jesus called Himself 'The Bread of Life' and said that anyone who fed on Him would live for ever.

Shortly before His death, Jesus shared His last meal with His disciples. He broke some bread with them, and drank some wine, and likened it to His body that would be broken for them, and His blood that would be spilled for them. Isaiah had prophesied that He would be despised, forsaken, whipped and broken for us.

Jesus instructed His disciples to continue to share this memorial meal with each other in the future to remind them of what He was doing for them. This is what we do in the Holy Communion.

48A

Bread of Life, Bread of Life,

God made man;

Taken, forsak'n,

Outcast, so I can

Take it, and eat it,

And make it for me;

And, partaking with others,

All may be set free!

John 6 v 47 – 51

Isaiah 53 v 3 - 12

Luke 22 v 7 – 20

49

Round and round the garden

Like a teddy bear.

One step, two steps!

Tickley under there.

This is simply a fun action rhyme, enjoyed by countless children for many years.

There was no fun and games in the garden around which Jesus wandered. He had left the last meal that He shared with His friends and went into a garden called Gethsemane. He hoped that He would be able to share with them some of the agony that He was going through in preparation for His death, but His disciples were tired and fell asleep. Jesus, left alone, cried bitter tears of anguish as He struggled with his desire to avoid the suffering ahead of Him. Finally, He submitted to God's will, and yielded to all that lay ahead of Him, in order to fulfil the plan God had for rescuing us.

49A

Round and round the garden,
Christ, a dread He bears;
One step, two steps,
Bitter tears and prayers.

Round and round the garden;
Friends, who said they'd share,
One step, two steps,
They sleep unaware.

Round and round the garden,
Christ, His steady prayer,
"Fulfill your will;
In your work I share."

Matthew 26 v 33 – 44

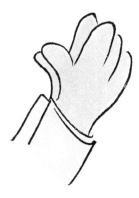

50

Jack and Jill climbed up the hill

To fetch a pail of water.

Jack fell down and broke his crown,

And Jill came tumbling after.

Up Jack got and home did trot

As fast as he could caper.

He went to bed to mend his head

With vinegar and brown paper

These lyrics possibly date back to the 17th century, when King Charles I tried to reform the taxes on liquid measures. When Parliament blocked this, he ordered that the volume of a Jack (1/2 pint) be reduced, but the tax retained, so he would still receive an increase in tax - hence 'Jack fell down and broke his crown'. Many pint glasses in the UK still have a line marking the 1/2 pint level with a crown above it. 'Jill' may have referred to a 'gill', or 1/4 pint, indicating that this too dropped in volume. Alcoholic beverages were often watered down, hence, 'fetch a pail of water.'

We all try to climb a different kind of hill - that of trying to be good enough for God, which, as we have seen throughout these songs, is impossible. We constantly fall down, and vinegar and brown paper will do nothing for the resulting broken lives! Christ alone was perfect and didn't deserve to die, and yet He was beaten and killed by men who could not accept His love. That love, though, was what eventually broke through all the evil and wrong doing of mankind, and Jesus' victory over death enables us to be forgiven and also to have victory.

Roman 7 v 18 - 19,   Galatians 3 v 10 - 11

Hebrews 4 v 15,   Matthew 27 v 29

John 11 v 47, 53,   1 Corinthians 15 v 24 - 28

Romans 3 v 23 - 24

50A

Jack and Jill climbed up the hill
Of 'doing what they oughta'.
Both fell down and broke their crowns,
And we came tumbling after.
We could not, no matter what,
Get past our first few capers.
For 'self' so led our heart and head;
To sin again's in our natures.

Christ fulfilled God's total will,
But man cried for his slaughter!
Beaten down, with thorny crown,
They led him stumbling after.
Shared this plot, "Now let's be shot
Of this man and His capers!
We've lost our cred through what He said,
This sinner man shan't escape us!"

When they killed Him on that hill
He bore the sin that thwarts us.
Then, Heav'n bound, with glory crowned,
Sent death a-tumbling after!
Sin that stopped us being what
We first of all were made for,
It fell instead on Jesus' head -
SO! Begin again - all is paid for!

...INNOCENT...

51

The Queen of hearts

She made some tarts

All on a summer's day.

The knave of hearts,

He stole those tarts

And took them clean away.

The King of hearts

Called for those tarts,

And beat the knave full sore.

The knave of hearts

Brought back the tarts,

And vowed he'd steal no more.

This rhyme was first printed in 1782, but has been immortalized by Lewis Carroll in his *Alice in Wonderland,* published in 1805. When annoyed by her servants the Queen of Hearts in the story was famous for the saying, "Off with their heads!"

The *odd song* tells of a battle between a king and the knave, but the *God song* is about the great battle between God and Satan, and how God, 'the King of hearts', longs for a love relationship with us. Satan, 'the knave of hearts' wants to spoil that relationship, and draw us away from God. Jesus, 'the Prince of hearts' was prepared to die in order to beat the knave, and, because Jesus rose, Satan can no longer have a lasting power over us.

51A

The King of hearts,

He makes new starts

For those who come His way.

The knave of hearts

Would spoil those starts

And looks to lead astray.

The Prince of Hearts,

Killed, but re-starts,

And beats the knave full sore.

The knave of hearts,

Thus beat, departs,

And power he wields no more.

2 Corinthians 5 v 17

1 Timothy 5 v 15

Romans 6 v 10

Revelations 20 v 2 - 3

52

This old man he played one

He played knick-knack on my drum.

With a knick-knack, Paddy-wack,

Give a dog a bone;

This old man came rolling home.

This old man he played two….three…..four…..etc

The origin of this rhyme is obscure, but it has clearly been used to help teach children to count.

When it comes to counting, the growth of the Christian church is a matter of multiplication, not addition! As more and more people heard the truth and were excited about what Jesus had achieved, so numbers grew rapidly.

When Jesus rose from the dead He met many different people, all astounded, but convinced that He was indeed alive! On one occasion He met two disciples walking home from Jerusalem, grieving that the One whom they thought would be their Saviour, had been killed and buried. He also appeared to the three women at the tomb after He had risen from the dead. They ran and told the disciples who spread the news around verbally, and later in the four Gospels and the Epistles. More than five hundred people saw Jesus after His resurrection, and the news spread like wild fire. We are now commissioned to continue to spread the good news, until there are millions who will be praising God.

52A

Our great God, He sent One,
He sent Jesus, His own Son,
So he'd bring back all who lack
Goodness of their own.
This God-Man will take us home.

When he'd risen, Christ met two
Walking home, depressed and blue;
And He shared that all the facts
As foretold were done,
Victory over death was won.

By the tomb, He met three,
Mary, Jo and James' mummy,
And they rushed back to the pack,
Said, "We're not alone!
God has rolled away the stone!"

Later on, there were four
Spread the news to many more
When they wrote that Gospel pack
Passed the message on,
Matthew, Mark and Luke and John.

52A *continued*

Paul then claimed there were five

Hundred, who'd seen Christ alive,

So we don't lack proof of fact

Death had been outdone,

And His risen life begun.

Six, seven, eight, nine and ten

Millions now can sing "Amen",

For we know that God has scrapped

All the wrong we've done;

Let's go out, tell everyone!

John 3 v 16

Luke 24 v 13 - 27

Luke 24 v 1 - 20

The Gospels of Matthew, Mark, Luke and John

1 Corinthians 15 v 6

Revelation 5 v 11

53

Humpty, Dumpty

Sat on the wall,

Humpty Dumpty

Had a great fall.

All the king's horses

And all the king's men

Couldn't put Humpty

Together again.

There is a theory that Humpty Dumpty was a large cannon used in the siege of Colchester in 1648 during the English Civil War. It was placed on the city wall and a shot from a Parliamentary cannon damaged the wall causing the cannon to fall. The Royalists, (all the King's men) attempted to raise Humpty Dumpty but failed - hence 'All the King's horses and all the King's men couldn't put Humpty together again!' This had drastic consequences for the Royalists as the strategically important town of Colchester fell to the Parliamentarians after a siege lasting eleven weeks. The earliest traceable publication of the rhyme is 1810.

The Good News of Jesus, or 'The Gospel', as it is called, is celebrated all through the New Testament, and it is described in many different ways. We have read of the lost being found, the thirsty being given water, the hungry being fed with bread, and here is yet another analogy, the broken being mended. Humpty Dumpty, whether we think of it as an egg shaped character or a huge cannon, fell and was broken, such that no-one could mend it. Our fall from all that God wants us to be is so catastrophic that nothing we do, no riches or cleverness, can ever restore us. That's why Jesus' message is such *Good News*. It tells us that He CAN mend us, and restore us as whole people back into a relationship with God.

53A

Humpty Dumpty!
Sadly we all,
Just like Humpty,
Had a great fall!
All our good causes
And all our wise men
Couldn't put us back
Together again.

Haughty, naughty!
Christ saw us fall.
Haughty, naughty!
Yet He loved all.
Bound evil forces
By dying and then,
Rising, He puts us
Together again

Romans 3 v 19 - 28

54

Oh! The grand old duke of York

He had ten thousand men.

He marched them up

To the top of the hill

And he marched them down again.

And when they were up they were up;

And when they were down they were down;

And when they were only half way up

They were neither up nor down!

This is believed to refer to Richard, Duke of York, heir to the English throne, and to the Battle of Wakefield in 1460. He and his army marched to his castle at Sandal and took up a defensive position against the Lancastrian army. Sandal Castle was built on top of the site of an old Norman fortress whose massive earthworks stood 10 metres above the original ground level ('he marched them up to the top of the hill'). In a moment of madness he left his stronghold in the castle and went down to make a direct attack on the Lancastrians, where he was killed and his army overwhelmed.

The 'Grand old Duke' went up and down the hill, and took his men with him. Jesus came down from Heaven in order to be able to take us back to Heaven with Him. And for those of us who find it all a bit of a struggle we can be encouraged by the fact that God will lift us up. It depends on Him, not on us. This is certainly something to sing about on earth, until we can sing about it again in Heaven!

54A

Oh! Our mighty God in Heav'n

He has so many men

Whose hearts go up

To their God – off'ring till

They can start in Heav'n again!

For those who are down can go up;

'Cos He who was up has come down;

And those who are struggling half way up

Will be raised right up from down!

Psalm 103 v 20 - 22

Psalm 104 v 33

Ephesians 2 v 4 - 6

Ephesians 4 v 8 - 10

Psalm 145 v 14

55

Hot cross buns!

Hot cross buns!

One a penny,

Two a penny,

Hot cross buns!

Tell it to your master,

Tell it to your sons.

One a penny,

Two a penny,

Hot cross buns.

In the 19th century hot cross buns were sold in the street to the cry of "Hot cross buns!" Now they are generally sold at Easter and commemorate the Easter Christian festival which celebrates the resurrection of Jesus following His crucifixion on the cross.

We are all familiar with hot cross buns, but, in the midst of pressing commercialism, we may have forgotten that the cross on the buns refers to the cross of Jesus, which brings us forgiveness. Now that is something worth telling our sons and daughters!

Hot cross buns!

Hot cross buns!

Tell of Heaven,

Sins forgiven;

Hot cross buns!

Tell it to your daughters,

Tell it to your sons.

Tell of Heaven,

Sins forgiven!

Hot cross buns!

Colossians 1 v 20, 23

56

Rub a dub dub

Three men in a tub;

And how do you think they got there?

The butcher, the baker,

The candlestick maker,

They all jumped out of a rotten potato.

'Twas enough to make a man stare.

The first recorded version of a similar rhyme is in *Christmas Box* published in London in 1798, though this refers to 'three maids in a tub'. It was traditional for one of the side shows at a local fair to include three unclothed ladies sitting in a bath! This rhyme is thought either to be scorning the young men who stared at them, or was a reference to three men who tried to get into the bath with them!

We don't know how the three odd gentlemen got into the tub, or why! But we do know that 'God's club', that is, all Christian believers, is made up of people of every class and race and social standing. Jesus came to make a way to God for EVERYONE. All it requires is a jump of faith into His arms, and He will take care of everything else.

56A

Rub a dub dub,

All sorts in God's club;

And how do you think they got there?

If butcher or baker,

From here or Jamaica,

They all jumped into the arms of their Maker

And trusted their lives to His care.

Galatians 3 v 28

Matthew 11 v 28

57

Simple Simon met a pie man

Going to the fair.

Said Simple Simon to the pie man,

"Let me taste your ware."

Said the pie man unto Simon,

"Show me first your penny!"

Said Simple Simon to the pie man,

"Sir, I have not any!"

In Medieval times, food was sold from trays at fairs by street sellers. This rhyme celebrates that custom.

Our culture is based on the understanding that commodities are bought and sold, just like the pie man's wares. Simon knew that if you haven't got money, then you can't have the goods. Many people feel that this must also be true of the way to get into Heaven. One must buy one's way in, if not with money, then with good works, or religious observance. Surely we must offer God SOMETHING in order to deserve a place in Heaven. There are many people who would love to be Christians, but don't feel good enough, or that they could never make the grade. Here is the good news; God's gift is free and offered to everyone, no matter how good or bad they are. It cannot be bought or earned. Christ bore the curse of our wrong doings, and He was the first to conquer death for us.

He tells us that He is our only hope as He is the only way to the Father

2 Corinthians 5 v 17 - 18

Romans 11 v 6

Galatians 3 v 13

Isaiah 53 v 5 - 6

John 14 v 6

160

57A

Troubled Tristan met a Christian
Going on in prayer.
Said troubled Tristan to the Christian,
"How can faith I share?"
Said the Christian unto Tristan,
"Not by work nor penny!"
Said Troubled Tristan to the Christian,
"But my sins are many!"

Troubled Tristan, met with Christian,
Bowed low in despair!
Said Troubled Tristan to the Christian,
"Sin's disgrace I bear!"
Said the Christian unto Tristan,
"Christ was cursed for many!"
Said troubled Tristan to the Christian,
"He can help me, can He?"

Troubled Tristan smiled at Christian,
Hope was in the air!
Said Troubled Tristan to the Christian,
"Can His grace I share?"
Said the Christian unto Tristan,
"Christ rose, first of many!"
Said Troubled Tristan to the Christian,
"*He's* my hope, if any!"

58

I went to the Animal Fair;

The birds and the beasts were there;

The big baboon by the light of the moon

Was combing his auburn hair.

The monkey fell out of his bunk,

Slid down the elephant's trunk.

The elephant sneezed and fell on his knees,

And what became of the monkey, monkey, monkey, monkey....?

It is very difficult to track down the origin of this camp fire song. It was probably just created for fun and humorous singing.

The square in Athens may well have had a lot in common with the 'Animal fair'! There would have been crowds of people of different nationalities, coming and going. There would have been a great hubbub with lots of noise and discussion, laughter and argument, just as there is wherever people get together to relax and pass the time of day!

We read about Athenean Square in *The Acts of the Apostles*, a book in the Bible that follows the Gospels. This book describes the activities of the early Christians, one of whom was Paul, an early convert to the message of Jesus. He couldn't stop talking about it. He was a very intelligent Jewish leader who debated the facts of Jesus' death and resurrection with great fervour in the Athenean Square, a place renowned for the gathering of philosophers and debaters. Some of them believed his message about Jesus, and others simply mocked him.

58A

Paul went to Athenian square;
He'd heard that they reasoned there!
From morn till noon, till the light of the moon,
They tossed ideas in the air.
They'd dip and they'd dive and they'd dunk;
Sorted the new from defunct;
But they weren't naive about what to believe,
And that's the way they all functioned, functioned, functioned,
functioned....

But Paul in Athenian square
New words and ideas did share.
They saw quite soon he was not a buffoon,
But argued his case with care.
Philosophers thought it was junk;
Tried all his claims to debunk;
But others were seized with such guilt, which was eased,
Confessing sin with compunction, punction, punction, punction....

'Cos down in Athenian square
They heard of God's peace right there.
"The One lampooned and then sent to his doom
Was killed and our sins did bear.
He rose and was seen by our bunch.
He came and talked and had lunch.
From death and disease and from sin he now frees
All those who work in conjunction, junction, junction, junction...."

Some folk in Athenian square
Who turned - were released in prayer;
Were then in tune and were over the moon
No longer were in despair;
Without Him they knew they were sunk;
Now with His joy they were drunk;
And God was so pleased that they're down on their knees,
And they were saved at this junction, junction, junction, junction....

Acts 17

59

Tom, Tom, the piper's son

Stole a pig and away did run.

The pig was eat

And Tom was beat,

And he went crying down the street.

'Piper's son' referred to any piper in the English Army or Navy. This rhyme clearly holds a moral lesson for all children. The origin of *Tom Tom the Piper's Son* dates back to the 18th century.

We can understand the concept of punishment for wrong doing such as stealing, even if we don't approve the method! The early Christians, however, were frequently beaten, not for doing wrong, but for sharing the wonderful truth of Jesus' love. Paul was beaten and left for dead, but continued to preach that Jesus was God's Son, who had died and risen again.

Jesus had warned His followers that if He, as their teacher and leader, was to suffer for the truth, so would they. This, however, in no way deterred them, but gave them added courage and determination. They were even prepared to be killed for the joy of being Jesus' followers.

Paul, Paul, a Jewish son

Spoke with vigour – proclaimed God's Son!"

This triggered heat

And Paul was beat;

Was left for dying on the street!

Paul, Paul, this Jewish son,

Bolder figure there ne'er was one.

No big retreat

But, on his feet,

Of Jesus' rising vowed he'd speak!

Acts 14 v 19 - 22

Acts 16 v 22 - 24

60

Two little dicky birds

Sitting on the wall;

One named Peter,

The other named Paul.

Fly away Peter!

Fly away Paul!

Come back Peter!

Come back Paul!

This little fun rhyme is used to amaze children with a trick of the fingers. Two 'dicky birds' (bits of paper on the tips of the index fingers) seem to disappear when the finger is lifted in the air. They then reappear next time. This is done by exchanging the first finger with the second, but most children do not notice the change over!

The Acts of the Apostles recounts many stories of the missionary work of another Peter and Paul. It tells how they travelled widely, spreading the good news. It is because of people like them that we have been able to hear of Jesus. Now the responsibility to share the Gospel with all nations of the world rests with those of us who already know. Jesus promised that He would be with those who take this responsibility seriously, and would meet their every need.

60A

Two willing missionaries
Listened for God's call;
One named Peter,
The other named Paul.
Read about Peter!
Read about Paul!
Their track records
In *Acts* fall.

More willing missionaries?
Is He calling you?
Might be better
Than filling the pew!
Why obey Jesus?
While you pray, you
Will lack nothing;
God backs you!

The Acts of the Apostles

Peter   *Chapters 2 – 5, 10, 11*

Paul   *Chapters 13, 14 – 28*

Matthew 28 v 19

61

This little piggy went to market;

This little piggy stayed at home;

This little piggy had roast beef,

And this little piggy had none;

And this little piggy went

"Wee wee wee", all the way home.

This little ditty can be traced back to 1728, and is just a fun way for adults to play with babies, playing with their toes and then tickling them all over.

It would seem that people, and therefore Christians, are no different from 'piggies'! There are those who are active and work, and there are those who stay at home for all sorts of different reasons. Some are well off, and have plenty to eat, whilst others are poor and hungry.

The early Christians were just the same, but they took Jesus' teaching very seriously. He had taught them to share everything they had so that no-one went without. Consequently they opened their homes and shared their possessions willingly and freely.

61A

This little Christian went to market;

This little Christian stayed at home;

This little Christian had roast beef,

But this little Christian had none!

So rich little Christian said,

"Please, please, please, eat at my home!"

Acts 2 v 44 - 46

62

Oh, dear! What can the matter be?

Dear, dear! What can the matter be?

Oh, dear! What can the matter be?

Johnny's so long at the fair.

He promised to buy me a basket of posies,

A garland of lilies, a garland of roses,

A little straw hat to set off the blue ribbons

That tie up my bonny brown hair.

This traditional song can be traced back as far as the 1700s in England, but nothing more is known of its origin.

Broken promises can bring so much heartache, but God never breaks His promises. He never said life would be easy for His followers, but He did promise to be with them through all the difficulties of life, to give them strength, and to turn the difficult times into times of growth and encouragement. Nothing can overcome His love, or His strength in them.

The Bible is full of examples of God's sustaining love in troubled times. This *God song* is an honest reflection of how we often feel down and fearful. It makes the bridge between the Old Testament writers who experienced so many trials, but who also knew the upholding power of God, and the New Testament writers who knew God's strength in an even more substantial way because of the death and resurrection of Jesus, and the gift of the Holy Spirit living in them. Despite our weaknesses and doubting, we can be assured that if we trust God, He *will* be with us through difficult times, and will bring us through them.

62A

Oh, dear! What can the matter be?
Fear has got to me latterly;
It's clear troubles just batter me;
God seems no longer to care!

He's promised He's by us when life's not all roses,
With calm He will fill us, a calm that transposes
My little, poor faith, and yes often blue moments,
With sighs of relief that He's there!

Oh, dear! So much can rattle me!
Dear, dear this is my battle, see,
I fear so much and that'll be
Why I'm all lost in despair!

We're told in the Bible, like Abram and Moses,
He guards us, instills us with peace that o'erflows us;
The prophets saw that they set off with new vision
When tied up to God's way in prayer.

62A *continued*

So, then! What can the matter be?
For, from Sunday to Saturday,
Life can't crush me or shatter me,
God is so strong in his care.

He promised that problems and dark days He uses
To grant us His stillness, our darkness defuses,
And as I draw back and let God give true wisdom
Then I in his purposes share.

Romans 8 v 28, 31, 35 - 38

Psalm 69 v 13 - 15

John 14 v 16 - 17

Genesis 15 v 1

Exodus 33 v 11, 14

Isaiah 55 v 8 - 9

Romans 5 v 3 - 4

63

Half a pound of tuppenny rice,

Half a pound of treacle.

That's the way the money goes,

Pop goes the weasel.

Up and down the City road,

In and out the Eagle,

That's the way the money goes,

Pop goes the weasel.

The bizarre words of this rhyme have led to many speculations about its origins, but one popular version is that it is steeped in Cockney rhyming slang and is believed to date back to the 1700s. Cockneys developed a language of their own based on a rhyming slang, such as 'stairs' being referred to as 'apples and pears'. In time the second half of the slang would be dropped, and the word substituted for stairs would be 'apples'. To 'pop' is the slang word for 'pawn' and 'weasel' is derived from 'weasel and stoat' meaning coat.

The belief is that poor people would pawn their best coat on Monday, and buy it back before Sunday - hence the term 'Pop goes the Weasel'.

'The Eagle' may refer to *The Eagle Tavern*, a pub which is located on the corner of City Road and Shepherdess Walk in Hackney, North London. *The Eagle* was an old pub which was re-built as a music hall in 1825, which was frequented by Charles Dickens (1812 - 1870). It was purchased in 1883 by the Salvation Army, which was totally opposed to drinking and music halls. The hall was later demolished and was rebuilt as a public house in 1901.

63A

Have you found you try to be nice,

But you've found you're evil?

That's the way I come and go,

Gosh! I'm so feeble!

Up and down! A pity, so!

Sin and doubt's so easy!

There's a way, just one to go,

Stop! Show me Jesus!

The poor folk probably intended to use their money wisely when they pawned their coats, but the temptation of the liqueur house was too great for them! They found that, although they tried to be good, they just couldn't make it!

As we move on to letters in the New Testament, written by the Apostles to the churches that had been established in the surrounding areas, we hear Paul confess to this self same dilemma. He wanted to do what was right, but couldn't, and he wanted not to do what was wrong, but still did it.

Paul realised that it was only Jesus who could deal with his wayward nature, and help him to win the battles. He talks about this in his letter to the Roman church.

Romans 7 v 14 – 8 v 1

64

If you're happy and you know it, clap your hands,

If you're happy and you know it, clap your hands,

If you're happy and you know it,

Then your really ought to show it,

If you're happy and you know it, clap your hands,

This is a popular children's song, which stems from an old Latvian folk song.

If we have experienced the amazing fact of God's forgiveness, two things should follow; our lives should be changed, and we should be eager to tell others of the great love of God. The New Testament letters are full of encouragement to share the Good News with others.

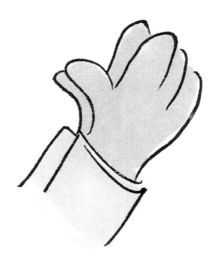

64A

If Christ's saved you and you know it, share His love!

If Christ's saved you and you know it, share His love!

If Christ's saved you and you know it,

Then your life should always show it;

If Christ's saved you and you know it, share His love.

If Christ's saved you and you know it, tell your friends;

If Christ's saved you and you know it, tell your friends;

If Christ's saved you and you know it,

Then to all your friends you owe it;

If Christ's saved you and you know it, tell your friends.

Romans 12 v 2

Romans 10 v 14 - 15

Romans 12 v 9 - 10

65

Jack Sprat could eat no fat;

His wife could eat no lean;

And so between them both, you see,

They licked the platter clean.

This nursery rhyme was apparently first published in 1639.

The Jack alluded to is thought to be Charles I, and his wife, Henrietta Maria. When King Charles declared war on Spain, Parliament refused to finance him (leaving him lean!). The King dissolved Parliament, and his wife imposed an illegal war tax (to get some fat!)

It is also thought that Jack Sprat (or Prat) was the 16th and 17th century name for a dwarf, and it is possible that his rhyme was written about a dwarf and his normal-sized wife.

Jack Sprat and his wife worked very well together! What one couldn't do, the other did, and vice versa. Paul likened the church to a body, with its many parts, that are interdependent on each other. He explains that when everyone is using his own individual gifts, the whole church functions properly.

65A

Fleet feet can eat no meat,
And eyes can never talk.
The nose between them cannot see,
And ears can never walk.

Ears hear and eyes can peer;
We need the nose to smell;
And so between them all, you see
The body functions well.

That's fact, and also that
On other folk we lean.
And so between us all, you see,
We make the perfect team!

1 Corinthians 12 v 12 - 27

66

Little Miss Muffet

Sat on a tuffet

Eating her curds and whey.

Along came a spider

Who sat down beside her

And frightened Miss Muffet away.

There is a theory that Miss Muffet was Patience, the daughter of Dr Thomas Muffet, a 16th century entomologist (someone who studies insects), who had a particular interest in arachnoids (spiders).

The 'tuffet' on which she sat was probably a small mound of earth but it was also the name of a three legged stool. Curds and whey are a kind of junket formed from milk, the thick part being the curds, and the runnier, watery part being the whey.

Some believe the verse to be symbolic of Mary Queen of Scots (1542 - 1587) and John Knox (1505 - 1572) (the spider), a minister who wanted to scare her off the throne because of their religious differences.

Miss Muffet was frightened by the spider, but we could easily be frightened by the sinister activities of the devil, who comes to disturb us when we least expect him.

Peter, in one of his letters, and Paul, in his letter to the Ephesians, warns us of the spiritual battle in which we are engaged, and how eager the devil is to confuse and mislead us. But we don't need to be frightened, for God is much more powerful that he is. One of the strategies against him, and one which Jesus used when He was tempted, was to quote Scripture at him. This makes him run!

66A

Little Miss Muffet
Sat on a tuffet;
Reading God's Word, she'd pray.
The devil beside her
Tried hard to misguide her
And frighten Miss Muffet away.

Little Miss Muffet
Sat on a tuffet;
Reading God's Word, she'd pray.
She'd quote from inside it,
Such strength it provided,
It frightened the devil away!

1 Peter 5 v 8

Ephesians 6 v 17

Matthew 4 v 1 - 11

Psalm 119 v 11

67

Itsy Bitsy spider

Climbing up the spout.

Down came the rain

And washed the spider out.

Out came the sunshine

And dried up the rain.

Itsy Bitsy spider

Climbed up the spout again.

The most commonly referenced first published version of this rhyme was in 1962. However, earlier references can be found in *Western Folklore* by the *Californian Society (1947)*. An alternative rendering is *Insey Winsey spider*.

It is fun for children to sing using hand movements.

Here's this wretched spider again! This time we could liken it to our pride, and all that's inside us that fights against God. We think we've got rid of it, and back it comes again!

Very often it is our pride that stops us allowing God to reign in our lives, and, try as we might, we seem to be unable to deal with it! The only answer is to give it to God, and allow him to wash us clean. He has promised that He will transform us, and make us more humble and more like Him if we will offer ourselves to him, pride and all! Several of the Epistles talk about this.

67A

It's a bit of pride here,

I'm not up to doubt,

Now claims the reins

And squashes Jesus out!

With shame, for some time

I've tried hard, in vain!

It's this bit of pride - it

Climbs in and spouts again!

It's this bit inside me

I must do without,

God can then reign

And wash the pride all out.

Now in His Son I'll

Abide and remain!

And this bit inside me

I'm offering God again.

Colossians 2 v 18 - 19

Philippians 2 v 3 - 4

1 Corinthians 15 v 25

Romans 12 v 1 - 2

68

Rock a bye baby

On the tree top,

When the wind blows the cradle will rock;

When the bough breaks the cradle will fall,

Down will come baby, cradle, and all.

This rhyme is reputedly from the custom of American Indian mothers hanging their babies in cradles from a tree whilst they were working in the fields.

The English history of the words relates to a family called the Kenyons who lived in a tree house which was formed within a massive yew tree nearly 2000 years old. They were charcoal burners from Shining Cliff Woods, Ambergate, Derbyshire in the 1700s. They had eight children and a tree bough was hollowed out to act as a cradle for their children! The Yew tree still exists but was severely fire damaged by vandals in the 1930s.

Jesus was also a baby once. And He was rocked to sleep by his mother, Mary, but this was no ordinary baby. When He was born, our fears were over, for He was, in fact, Lord of the universe, victor over death, evil and Satan.

In two of his letters, that to the Corinthians, and that to the Colossians, Paul rejoices at this victory that Jesus has won. The promise was there when He was born as a baby in Bethlehem, and Satan's power was broken when He died and rose again. The earth itself rocked then as a sign of Christ's victory. Total destruction of death and evil will be experienced when He comes again in glory!

68A

Rock the Christ Baby,

Here our fears stop!

When His wind blows the earth it will rock;

When His power breaks, old Satan will fall,

Down will come evil, death, sin and all.

Matthew 27 v 50 - 53

Acts 2 v 2

1 Corinthians 15 v 54 - 57

Colossians 2 v 15

69

Polly put the kettle on!

Polly put the kettle on!

Polly put the kettle on!

We'll all have tea.

Sukie take it off again!

Sukie take it off again!

Sukie take it off again!

They've all gone home!

Molly Put the Kettle On was published by Joseph Dale in London in 1803. It was also printed with 'Polly' instead of 'Molly' in Dublin about 1790 – 1810.

There is also the theory that the author had five children, two boys and three girls and that there were constant arguments as the boys wanted to play soldiers and the girls wanted to play house! When the girls wanted to play without their brothers they would pretend to start a game of tea party and the daughter, called Polly, would put the toy kettle on! As soon as the brothers left, Sukey (or Susan) would take it off again! Their father was so amused by this ploy that he set it to words and music and it was subsequently published.

Once again, in our *God song*, we see a battle going on - not between brothers and sisters, but between the followers of Jesus, and His arch enemy, the devil. Satan quakes with fear when we read the Bible, because he knows that it holds the truth, and Jesus tells us that "the truth will set you free!"

We are reminded of the importance of getting to know Scripture, both to thwart Satan, and to read of God's offer to bring us back home to Him. Paul reminds Timothy of this in his letter to him.

69A

Polly get the Bible out!

Polly get the Bible out!

Polly get the Bible out!

We all will see!

Satan quakes with wrath again;

Satan quakes with wrath again;

Satan quakes with wrath again;

"That *awful* tome!"

Polly get the Bible out!

Polly get the Bible out!

Polly get the Bible out!

It calls to me!

Should we take its offer then?

Should we take its offer then?

Should we take its offer then?

And all 'come home'!

1 Timothy 4 v 13

Genesis 3 v 1

2 Timothy 3 v 16 - 17

70

Diddle, diddle dumpling

My son John

Went to bed with his trousers on!

One shoe off and one shoe on.

Diddle, diddle dumpling, my son John.

This rhyme is recorded when printed in *The Newest Christmas Box in London* around 1797.

Hot dumpling sellers in old London town used to cry out "Diddle Diddle Dumpling!" when selling their wares. The John in this rhyme sounds as though he may have been a bit diddled (drunk!) the night before, and probably not from eating dumplings!

I guess going to bed a little bit 'diddled' may well not harm anyone, even if it leads to being somewhat ridiculous! On the other hand, it may lead to a loosening of the tongue, which can have very serious consequences!

James, in his letter, warns of the dangers of the tongue. What a lot of harm can be done by such a small part of the body!

70A

Tittle tattle, grumbling,

Lies are spun;

Rumours spread, and the row's begun;

Peace is off and war is on!

Did all this all come from my small tongue?

James 3 v 2 - 12

71

Goosey, goosey gander

Whither will you wander?

Upstairs, downstairs,

In my lady's chamber.

There I met an old man

Who wouldn't say his prayers.

I took him by the left leg

And threw him down the stairs.

Details of the origin of this ditty can be found with rhyme number 12, where, in the *God song* we learnt of the way the Israelites wavered between following Baal and Jehovah.

In this *God song* we learn how easy it is for us to be uncertain whom we really want to follow.

James warns us to take truth seriously, and not to waiver from it or take on board anything that just takes our fancy. He emphasises the need to be consistent. Jesus taught how important it is to meet with God in prayer, in a quiet place, to hear what He is saying, and Timothy tells us that we can find the truth in Scripture. Here, therefore, are two ways to guard against meandering from one point of view to another.

71A

You see you meander,
Willing to be fonder
Of peers' ideas,
Truth you'll maybe squander.
If you met an old man,
And foolish ways he shares,
You'd shift from right to left leg;
For truth - who really cares?

Truth you see, *I* ponder,
Wishing *not* to wander.
God shares my cares
In my inner chamber.
There I met with 'God-Man'
Who listened to my prayers,
I took the Bible - was led
To truth, as it declares.

James 1 v 6

Matthew 6 v 6 - 7

2 Timothy 3 v 16

72

Peter Piper picked a peck of pickled pepper;

A peck of pickled pepper Peter Piper picked.

If Peter Piper picked a peck of pickled pepper

Where's the peck of pickled pepper

That Peter Piper picked?

The earliest version of this tongue twister was published in *Peter Piper's Practical Principals of Plain and Perfect Pronunciation* by John Harris, London, in 1813. It includes one name tongue twister for each letter of the alphabet, in the same style.

This one was, however, known at least a generation earlier.

The *God song* is another 'Peter' tongue twister!

Peter wrote two letters to the early churches, and this tongue twisting ditty summarises the main content of the first one. It reminds us that the words are not meant to stay on the paper, but their truths are meant to be evident in the lives of Jesus' followers.

72A

"Postle Peter penned a pair of pep epistles;

A pair of pep epistles Apostle Peter penned.

If 'postle Peter penned a pair of pep epistles,

What's the pick of precious pond'rings

Apostle Peter penned?

1 Peter 5 v 12

'Postle Peter preached of patient perseverance;

Of patient perseverance Apostle Peter preached.

If 'postle Peter preached of patient perseverance,

Where's the patient perseverance

Apostle Peter preached?

1 Peter 1 v 6 - 7

'Postle Peter preached of power protecting people;

Of power protecting people, Apostle Peter preached;

If 'postle Peter preached of power protecting people,

Where's the power protected people

T'whom 'postle Peter preached?

1 Peter 1 v 5

'Postle Peter preached of peace through pain that passes;

Of peace through pain that passes Apostle Peter preached;

If 'postle Peter preached of peace through pain that passes,

Where's the people's peace and patience

Apostle Peter preached?

1 Peter 4 v 7, 14

'Postle Peter preached of priestly people;

Of priestly people Apostle Peter preached;

If 'postle Peter preached of priestly people,

Where's the priestly people

T' whom Apostle Peter preached?

1 Peter 2 v 9

'Postle Peter preached of precious, pard'ning passion

Of precious, pard'ning passion Apostle Peter preached.

If 'postle Peter preached of precious pard'ning passion,

Where have penitential people

Poured out praise 'cos not impeached?

1 Peter 1 v 18 - 19,

1 Peter 2 v 4,

1 Peter 4 v 16

73

Daisy, Daisy,

Give me your answer do!

I'm half crazy, all for the love of you.

It won't be a stylish marriage;

I can't afford a carriage;

But you'll look sweet upon the seat

Of a bicycle made for two!

For the history of this rhyme see rhyme number 7.

The love of Daisy's suitor is nothing compared with the love God has for us, which led Him to die for us in a cruel and horrendous manner.

The book of Jude is a very short letter written by Jesus' younger brother to a church that was threatened by false teaching.

He warns them of the dangers, and challenges them to remain faithful. He concludes his letter with a powerful reminder of the glory and authority of God who, because of what Jesus has done for them, can bring them, perfect, into His presence. Isaiah, centuries previously, had spelt out so vividly the anguish that the Messiah would have to face in order to for us to be 'counted righteous'. That Jesus should be prepared to do that for us is certainly something to praise and give Him glory for.

73A

Praise Him, praise Him,

Give Him His honour due!

It's amazing – all of his love for you!

Now all that is vile is vanquished,

Your sin He bore in anguish!

With joy He'll greet you when you meet;

What a price He has paid for you!

Jude v 24 - 25

Isaiah 53 v 1 - 12

74

Pease porridge hot,

Pease porridge cold,

Pease porridge in the pot

Nine days old.

Some like it hot,

Some like it cold,

Some like it in the pot,

Nine days old.

The earliest known publication of this rhyme was in 1760, in John Newbery's *Mother Goose's Melody,* and refers to a type of porridge made from peas.

Just as pease porridge can be hot or cold, so can our love for God.

The book of *Revelation* is the last book in the Bible. It describes a vision had by John, of the battle between God and Satan, and the eventual victory won through Jesus. In it there are various messages sent to the churches by the angels. Here God warns one of the churches that they have become lukewarm in their love for Jesus, and that He will reject them. He does, however, offer them 'gold' in place of this lukewarm allegiance to Him.

74A

Some churches hot,

Some churches cold,

Some Christians' love has got

Tired and old.

When it's not hot

Nor is it cold,

God rejects what they've got,

Off'ring gold.

Revelation 3 v 14 - 22

75

"Oranges and lemons,"
Say the bells of St Clements.
"You owe me five farthings,"
Say the bells of St Martin's.
"When will you pay me?"
Say the bells of Old Bailey.
"When I grow rich,"
Say the bells of Shorditch.
"When will that be?"
Say the bells of Stepney?
"I do not know!"
Says the great bell of Bow.

Here comes the candle to light you to bed.
And here comes a chopper to chop off your head.
Chip chop! Chip chop! The last man's dead!

75A

"How is it love left us?"

Ask the bells in Eph-es-us.

"Our love has grown firmer."

Say the bells back in Smyrna.

"False ways corrupt some."

Say the bells of Perga-mum.

"Don't follow 'HER"

Tolls out Thyatira.

"In the abyss!"

Say the bells of Sardis.

"You persevere!"

Tolls out Philadelphia.

"Here comes a visitor, Laodicea!

Yes here comes His knocking; it's gentle but clear.

Knock, knock! Knock, knock! Your Master's here!

The exact date of origin here is unknown but there was a Square Dance called *Oranges and Lemons* dating back to 1665. The neighbourhood names relate to some of the many churches of London and the tune that accompanies the lyrics emulates the sound of the ringing of the individual church bells.

The words of the nursery rhyme are chanted by children as they play the game of *Oranges and Lemons,* which culminates in a child being caught between the joined arms of two others, enacting their heads being chopped off!

The last three lines of the lyrics were added to the original rhyme some time before 1783 when the infamous public execution gallows (the Tyburn-tree) was moved from Tyburn Gate (Marble Arch) to Newgate. There was a notorious prison there for both criminals and debtors. The line 'When will you pay me?' alludes to the debtors.

The 'Bells of Old Bailey', or more accurately the tenor bell of St Sepulchre, had been used prior to 1783 to time the executions. After the gallows had been moved, Newgate prison (now the site of the Old Bailey) obtained its own bell. The executioner would inform his victim on death row of their impending doom by tolling the 'Execution Bell' (a large hand bell at St Sepulchre) on the Sunday night preceding their execution. The actual executions commenced at nine o'clock Monday morning, following the first toll of the tenor bell.

In the traditional rhyme, the bells of London toll out their sober messages. In this *God song* the bells of the 7 new churches toll out the messages given to John in his revelation.

This is a very brief summary of the messages, some praising their faithfulness, and others giving very severe warnings of what would happen if they failed to repent and change their ways.

You will need to chant the rhythm of the bells, as in the original rhyme, to appreciate the rhythm of the *God song*!

<u>Ephesus</u>
Revelation 2 v 4

<u>Smyrna</u>
Revelation 2 v 9 - 10

<u>Pergamum</u>
Revelation 2 v 14 – 15

<u>Thyatira</u>
Revelation 2 v 20 – 21

<u>Sardis</u>
Revelation 3 v 1 - 3

<u>Philadelphia</u>
Revelation 3 v 8 – 12

<u>Laodicea</u>
Revelation 3 v 20

76

She'll be coming round the mountain when she comes;

She'll be coming round the mountain when she comes;

She'll be coming round the mountain,

She'll be coming round the mountain,

She'll be coming round the mountain when she comes.

This song, believed to have been written during the late 1800s, was based on an old Negro spiritual, *When the Chariot Comes,* sung to the same melody. It is not known who the 'she' was, but it may have been the train that would come along the tracks being laid by the workers.

The original Negro spiritual looked forward to Christ's return, talked about by Old Testament prophets and Jesus Himself. This final *God song* sums up what we can know about that day from the Bible.

Zechariah tells us that the Messiah will stand on the Mount of Olives when He finally comes, and the mountain will split in two. (*Zechariah 14 v 3 – 7)*

Jesus tells us that the prophets of old longed to see the day of the Messiah about which they preached, and, in Mark's Gospel He tells us there will be many false prophets beforehand, and many wars, earthquakes and famines, and that the sun and moon will be darkened. Everyone will see the Son of Man coming on the clouds with great power and glory. (*Matthew 13 v 17 and Mark 13 v 5 – 27)*

Paul warns us in *Romans* that we will have to give an account of ourselves. (*Romans 14 v 11 – 12)*

In *Revelation*, we read that we will only be saved if our names are written in the Book of Life. (*Revelation 20 v 15)*

Zechariah talks of a fountain that will cleanse God's people from all their sins. (*Zechariah 13 v 1 - 3)*

It is clear that the great day will actually come when we are least expecting it, and we need to be ready at all times!

76A

He will come to Olive Mountain when He comes;
And on coming split the mountain when He comes;
And the prophets who've been shouting
Will see what 'twas all about in
That great day upon the mountain when He comes.

There'll be floods, and wars and routing ere He comes;
And false prophets will be touting ere He comes;
There'll be earthquakes in the mountains
Till the sun and moon go out in
All the troubled days surrounding when He comes.

There will come the great accounting when He comes;
Will you somehow still be doubting when He comes?
Will you God's will still be flouting,
Will your works God be discounting,
Will your sins have just been mounting till He comes?

Will you thank Him for his bounty when He comes?
Will your name be one that's counted when He comes?
Will your sins be all rubbed out in
That great day upon the mountain
'Cos you're washed in Jesus' fountain when He comes?

Other books by Dr Hazel Butler

Heaven's Humpties

Book and CD

Available from: www.whole-in-one.org.uk